Advance Praise for Ecological Design and Building Schools

A current and comprehensive resource covering the scope of offerings in sustainable design education today. This book also traces the history and evolution of practical training in sustainable design, serving the student, practitioner, and educator.

– Margot McDonald, AIA
Professor of Architecture. Cal Poly, San Luis Obispo

If you want to learn more about ecological design and building education this is the book you need. Up to now finding the right program has been extremely frustrating. This guide simplifies the process with clear diagrams and excellent descriptions that cut through the sales hyperbole and help you find the learning environment that best fits your needs.

– Antony Brown
Director, Ecosa Institute

Given our dwindling oil reserves and delicate ecosystems, in the very near future ecological design and building will be the only way to go. Nary a week goes by that our firm doesn't hear from an aspiring student of architecture, asking what schools are best to help create a sustainable future. Finally, we have a guide to point them to. Besides thorough listing and comparison of programs, this book's coverage of history and current state of green building make it valuable to all design and building professionals, not just students.

– David Arkin, AIA
Arkin Tilt Architects

As "sustainability" becomes a more popular topic and green coursework appears in more institutions, it is difficult for the uninitiated to discern between shallow and deep programs. Few tools could be more important than this book at this time.

– Jason F. McLennan
Principal, BNIM Architects

FRONT COVER VISUALS

Top row:

Students engaged in discussion during outdoor session at The Farm. (2004)
Photographer: Albert Bates, Global Village Institute

Symbiosis Model for changes to the architecture profession related to sustainability.
Courtesy of EASE

Schematic drawing of solar path in the northern hemisphere.
Courtesy of National Renewable Energy Laboratory

Green roof atop Chicago's City Hall.
Courtesy of National Renewable Energy Laboratories

Second row:

Yestermorrow student taking measurements of roof beams. (April 2004)
Courtesy of Yestermorrow

Seminar held in one of Cal-Earth's ceramic structures.
Courtesy of CAL-Earth

Model of University of Texas at Austin entry to 2002 Solar Decathlon.
Courtesy of National Renewable Energy Laboratory

Third row:

Student at PANGEA applies earth plaster to straw bale walls.
Courtesy of PANGEA

Planning study layering ecological data for Boggy Creek
Courtesy of University of Texas at Austin.

Students working on ECOSA Housing project at the ECOSA studio. (November 2003)
Photographer: Megan Clark

SEI photovoltaic panel installation training course.
Courtesy of Solar Energy International

University of Virginia entry to 2002 Solar Decathlon under construction.
Courtesy of National Renewable Energy Laboratory

Ecological Design and Building Schools

Green Guide to Educational Opportunities in the United States and Canada

Sandra Leibowitz Earley

NEW VILLAGE PRESS
Oakland California

Ecological Design and Building Schools:
Green Guide to Educational Opportunities in the United States and Canada

Front cover and graphic design by Megan Clark.

Printed in Canada.
First printing, October 2005.

The text of this book is printed on 60# Rolland Enviro 100, an acid-free,
recycled paper made of 100% post consumer waste.
No trees have been cut to produce this paper.

Paperback
10-digit ISBN: 0-9766054-1-4
13-digit ISBN: 978-0-9766054-1-6

Library of Congress Control Number: 2005930903

To order copies of this book directly from the publisher please add US$5.00 shipping to the price of the book (for additional copies add $2.00/each). California residents add appropriate state sales tax. Send check or money order to New Village Press.

New Village Press
P.O. Box 3049
Oakland, CA 94609
(510) 420-1361
press@newvillage.net
www.newvillagepress.net

New Village Press books are published under the auspices of
Architects/Designers/Planners for Social Responsibility.
www.adpsr.org

Table of Contents

Acknowledgements

It is commonly said that "I could not have done this alone," yet in this case the statement could not be more truthful. This book owes the greatest thanks to the skillful research, tenacious contact management, and impressive graphic design talents of research assistant Megan Clark, who worked with me on this project for one and half years from early 2004 through the summer of 2005. Great appreciation is also due to the early research, database development, and organizational wisdom of intern Eli Zigas who helped me revive this project during the summer of 2003, nearly seven years after the release of Eco-Building Schools, Fall 1996. To both Eli and Megan, I express still further gratitude for their enthusiasm and passion for the importance of this subject.

I also give sincere thanks to Lynne Elizabeth, ADPSR colleague and friend whose insight and professional perspective for this project led to a productive publishing relationship with a social mission. To Sigi Koko, ecological design colleague and friend, my deepest appreciation for her thoughtful peer reviews. Thank you to those who supported and inspired my original research endeavors back in Oregon in the mid 1990s, and all of the motivated groups and individuals doing the good work, past and present, that this book exists to showcase. Finally, I thank my wise and wonderful husband Chris Earley, whose support for what is important to me helps me be strong every day.

Preface

This book is about educational opportunities and resources. It includes information on subtly different variations of what may be called ecological design, green architecture, green building, building science, natural building and sustainable design. I do not draw hard boundaries among the different terms, as often the industry itself is not sure where to draw those lines. This book is also not about rating or ranking schools and resources. Rather, it is providing information readers can use to make their own decisions about educational pursuits. This book offers as many of the viable educational options as could be found in the scope of my investigation, holds up examples to emulate, and presents the story of how ecological design and building education arrived where it is today.

The movement in college and university architecture and related design programs toward ecological education has brought with it a high profile, industry esteem, and some funding. Furthermore, new requirements from the National Architectural Accrediting Board (NAAB) explicitly include sustainable design as a core competency for architecture school accreditation, which draws even greater attention to the need for this material within architectural curricula. Indeed, the amount of academic and professional attention paid to this subject in the last 20 years, and especially the last five to ten years, inspired me to include a chapter on recent educational initiatives.

This book is influenced by my education, my recent professional experience, and observations of the field of sustainable design education. Having determined in 1992 that sustainable architecture was the only path in architecture I was willing to pursue, I chose the University of Oregon School of Architecture and Allied Arts and its Master of Architecture program, appreciating that it chose me as well. There I found a community impressively supportive of ecological design.

Though very satisfied by the formal instruction at the University of Oregon, I grew fascinated by alternative educational resources and began to explore them. From this I developed a paper on educational resources outside of architecture schools for a spring 1994 "Environmental Resources Design" seminar. In fall 1996, I self-published a 20-page guide entitled *Eco-Building Schools: A Directory of Alternative Educational Resources in Environmentally Sensitive Design and Building in the United States*. I also produced a companion website co-sponsored by the Ecological Design Institute.

Having benefited from a healthy combination of formal instruction and continuing education, I set about an alternative, environmental career in what is known commercially as sustainable design or green building. Engaged in consulting on project teams and researching environmentally preferred technologies, I immersed myself in this demanding work, eventually launching my own consulting business. Along the way I was privileged to contribute to several directories and guidance documents on a variety of green building topics, which provided me an important outlet to share my research and experience.

In 2003, I attended the University of Oregon's H.O.P.E.S. Conference, where a roundtable on ecological design education caught my attention. Students, faculty and professionals were comparing the integration of ecological design concepts into formal architecture degree programs with interdisciplinary certificate programs in ecological design. This discussion and the entire conference reminded me of the important transfer of knowledge between the practitioner sectors and the educational sectors and reignited my passion to investigate ecological design and building education. So, back in my East Coast office, with a research intern on board, I began the job of developing this book.

This book's audience includes students just entering higher education, professionals mid-career in design or related fields, and those from unrelated fields who are seeking a new vocation in the growing green building movement. This book will also surely be valuable to educators, who are curious about what their peers are teaching and who wish to broaden their understanding of the field. Very recent requirements to include sustainability in formal design school curriculum are also changing simple curiosity about what's being taught into an imperative to revise it.

Readers should appreciate the book's unique descriptions of ecological design and building course content, sample course formats, and initiatives. Students, educators and design and building professionals will likely find the 20-year history of green design illuminating to their studies and practice. Not being primarily an educator, myself, but rather a fascinated observer and life-long student, I have chosen to present the information I collected in a practical, easy-to-use format, instead of in a formal academic report.

Since this book's audience is broad, the content has multiple dimensions, and some dimensions will apply more directly to what an individual reader seeks than others. The impetus for placing straw-bale workshops in the same book with daylighting seminars, and passive-solar home design classes with formal degree programs in sustainable architecture, stems from appreciating the benefits I myself derived from such diversity as a student and professional. And so, this guidebook includes architecture and design schools, professional development programs, and non-professional continuing education and owner-builder programs, as well as additional resources.

I invite readers to approach this book with an open mind, to take advantage of the diversity of resources, and to recognize that their educational options in ecological design and building continue to grow each day. Those looking to begin a new career path should be encouraged by the abundance of opportunities, while educators themselves may take advantage of this book to evaluate and improve the quality and variety of their own offerings.

Recent Educational Initiatives

1

"The underlying premise is that education is a key part of creating awareness and demand for green buildings, and enhancing the ability of design professionals to deliver them. Since the environmental values that students hold while at architectural school typically stay with them throughout their professional lives, this transformation must logically begin with reassessing design education."

– Daniel Pearl

Recent Educational Initiatives

Ecological design and building education has roots in traditional indigenous building knowledge, in early 20th century modern and organic movements, and in the solar energy renaissance of the 1970s and early 1980s. These roots, while essential, have not led as directly to the current forms of ecological design and building education as have recent educational initiatives, organized here in a timeline of the last twenty years.

Foresight in the Early Years

Taking cues from the solar energy movement, and even more specifically, the passive solar design movement, the Society of Building Science Educators (SBSE) held its first meeting at the University of New Mexico's School of Architecture in September 1983. By 1986 SBSE was funded and held its first curriculum development retreat at Heceta Head in Oregon. SBSE's goal of promoting and supporting quality instruction in building science is realized through a broad range of practical activities and the ongoing facilitation of individual member's teaching projects at their home institutions. Though a relatively low-profile organization, SBSE's membership stretches across the U.S. and internationally, and its members have founded or participated in many of the other educational initiatives represented in this chapter throughout the last two decades.

The early 1990s set the tone for a new international environmental movement. At the United Nations Conference on Environment and Development (UNCED), held June 1992 in Rio de Janeiro, sustainability was elevated to a primary international agenda. This conference, commonly known as the Earth Summit, also addressed economic opportunity, social equity, and environmental responsibility on global and local scales.

1982

Society of Building Science Educators (SBSE) established

1982 1983 1984 1985

In 1993, a pivotal World Architecture Congress held in Chicago placed environmental and social sustainability at the core of architectural responsibilities. It featured the signing of a "Declaration of Interdependence for a Sustainable Future" by presidents of the International Union of Architects (UIA) and the American Institute of Architects (AIA) as well as several thousand congress participants. The event demonstrated that architects and others in the building industry had begun to make the connection between their professional work and the well-being of the planet and its inhabitants. This momentum soon led to the formation of two prolific organizations in the United States: the American Institute of Architects Committee on the Environment (AIA COTE) and the U.S. Green Building Council (USGBC).

Expanding Activities in the Mid-1990s

Meanwhile, at the University of Oregon, graduate architecture students transformed a funding-starved, formerly faculty-run research program known as the Solar Energy Center into the Solar Information Center (SIC). This new interdisciplinary student organization (housed simultaneously in the Departments of Architecture, Environmental Studies, and Physics) provided students, faculty and the larger community with a popular resource center, library, ongoing lecture and workshop series and a quarterly newsletter, Solar Incidents. Solar Incidents showcased student research and studio work in ecological design, and its Fall 1994 issue featured an early version of "Eco-Building Schools," my research into alternative educational resources outside of architecture schools. From 1994 to early 1996, while a graduate student at the University of Oregon, I co-directed the SIC in the company of other students who have since moved onto ecological architectural design and building careers.

In May 1994, thanks to the passion and energy of Marvin Rosenman, Chair of Ball State University Department of Architecture, and his colleagues, a new initiative was launched to "green" the architectural profession at its

Summer 1986

1st SBSE Curriculum Development Retreat at Heceta Head State Park, OR

1986 1987 1988 1989 1990

educational roots. This groundbreaking initiative – Educating Architects for a Sustainable Environment (EASE) – was funded by the U.S. Environmental Protection Agency Region 5 and others. It began with a planning conference in Cooper Landing, Alaska that called for "a reevaluation of program content in U.S. architectural education, in response to the demands of sustainable design principles, social equity and changing demographics, economic restructuring, available media and technologies, and the appropriateness of enabling architects and environmental designers to assume leadership positions in the world community."

At this first EASE Project event, invited participants, including faculty and students generated lists of recommendations in the following categories:

1. The Importance of Values and Ethics
2. The Relevance of Economics
3. The Need for a Knowledge base
4. A Re-examination of the Curriculum
5. A Relationship with the Community
6. Changes to the Profession
7. An Interdisciplinary Approach
8. Individual and Institutional Change

EASE Cooper Landing conference (May 1994)

Recommendations made at this event broadened the EASE Project's influence to a larger architectural education community, including a Teachers' Seminar on Sustainability and Design held June 1994 at the Cranbrook Academy in Bloomfield Hills, Michigan by the AIA and the U.S./Canadian Association of Collegiate Schools of Architecture (ASCA). At the Teachers' Seminar, additional recommendations were generated to supplement those from the first EASE Project planning conference.

The second planning conference of the EASE Project, held in May 1995, focused on the development of specific implementation strategies for

June 1992

Vital Signs Curriculum Materials Project coordinated by the Center for Environmental Design Research at the University of California, Berkeley

VITAL SIGNS

May 1994

1st Educating Architects for a Sustainable Environment (EASE) Planning Conference in Cooper Landing, Alaska

1994

The Cob Cottage Company orga the first "Alternative (Natural) Bu Colloquium" for builders and tea in Cottage Grove, Oregon

June 1994

Teachers' Seminar on Sustainab & Design sponsored by the AIA the Association of Collegiate Sc of Architecture (ACSA) at Cranb Academy, Bloomfield Hills, Mich

1991 | **1992** | 1993 | **1994**

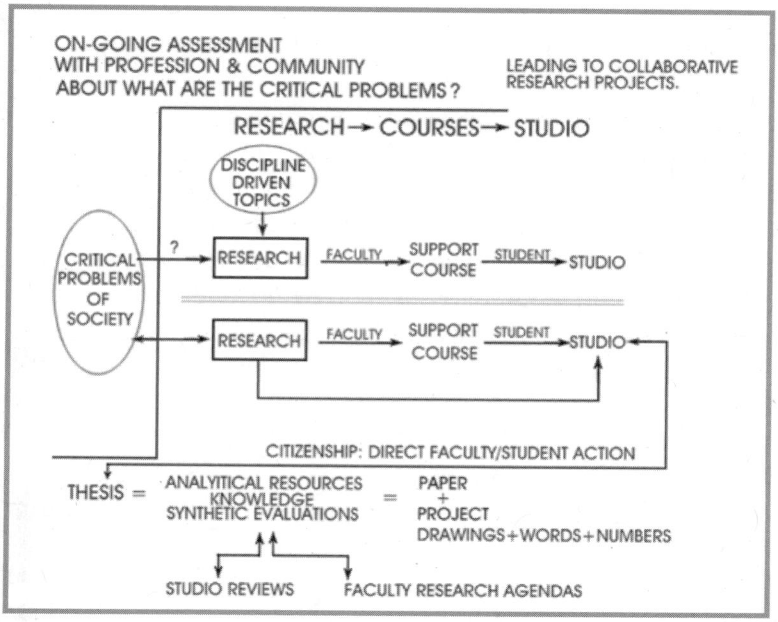

Knowledge-based Curriculum Model, differentiating the conventional way and an alternate model for undertaking research in schools of architecture. Courtesy of EASE

the EASE Recommendations and proposed model curricula to be built around these strategies. The intention of its creators was to integrate their work with similar ongoing endeavors in the design and building professions. The EASE Project ceased its activities in 1998 but left behind a legacy for others to carry forward, including documentation of its work and resources.

During the time EASE's exemplary work was developing under the leadership of architecture faculty, a unique student initiative emerged at the University of Oregon. A new student organization named Holistic Options for Planet Earth Sustainability (H.O.P.E.S.) formed in 1994 in the School of A&AA, representing not only the school's architecture program but its "allied arts" programs, as well. H.O.P.E.S. focused its all-volunteer student efforts, with faculty support and university funding, on organizing the first annual Eco-Design Arts Conference in April 1995. The conference, originally modeled after

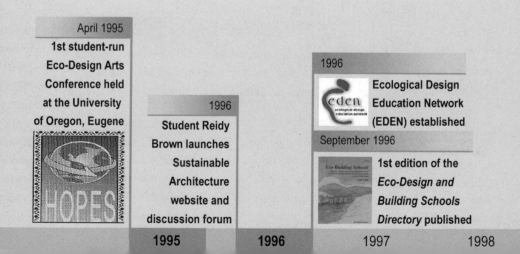

April 1995

1st student-run Eco-Design Arts Conference held at the University of Oregon, Eugene

1996

Student Reidy Brown launches Sustainable Architecture website and discussion forum

1996

Ecological Design Education Network (EDEN) established

September 1996

1st edition of the *Eco-Design and Building Schools Directory* published

1995 **1996** 1997 1998

the world-famous University of Oregon annual student-run Environmental Law Conference, became known simply as H.O.P.E.S.

Following the momentum built by the first H.O.P.E.S. conference, in January 1996 the Ecological Design Institute held a retreat in Bur Sur, California. The Ecological Design Institute was founded as a not-for-profit organization by pioneer eco-architect, educator and author Sim Van der Ryn to carry out innovative projects in sustainable design, education and research. This retreat focused on planning a new program to link architecture and design students to paid internships in the field of ecological design. The program was named Ecological Design Education Network (EDEN) and promptly launched a website that featured an Intern Recruiter tool "to allow professional offices and organizations to quickly identify and contact student intern candidates whose qualifications matched their needs." The site also hosted, among other resources, a summary version of my 1996 publication, *Eco-Building Schools*. With no further outside funding to support a continued effort, the EDEN project came to a halt in 1998.

Meanwhile, during 1996 and 1997, an Internet-savvy prospective architecture graduate student named Reidy Brown posted a website filled with her research into sustainable design education. Unique to this website was an archive of correspondence from architecture students and facility throughout the U.S. responding to Brown's own inquiries into graduate programs she was considering. Her forum provided one of the first compilations of student-oriented information on ecological architectural programs.

From 1996 through 1998, although partly funded in prior years, the College of Environmental Design at the University of California at Berkeley undertook a new project named Vital Signs. The overall goal of Vital Signs was "to incorporate matters of building physical performance into the education of architects" and to "instill in architecture students a fundamental awareness about the numerous ways in which their design decisions affect a building's physical performance -- from energy use, to indoor environmental quality, to occupant well-being."

2000
st Agents of Change Project funded by U.S. Department of Education

September 2000
ACSA *NEWS* published 1st of 7 sustainable design editorials by university educators
ACSA NEWS

August 2001
Second Nature held Education for Sustainability at Wingspred, Racine, Wisconsin

August 2002
"Greening the Curricula: Infusion of Environmental and Sustainability Issues in Canadian Schools of Architecture" Collogue at the Université de Montréal

September 2002
1st Solar Decathlon organized by the U.S. Department of Energy

March 2002
The Sustainable Environmental Design Education Project (SEDE) undertaken by the California Integrate Waste Managemen Board and the Renewable Energy Institute at Cal-Pol San Luis Obispo

1999 | 2000 | 2001 | 2002

As a key element of the Vital Signs project, U.S. and Canadian architectural faculty developed a series of flexible, modular "Resource Packages" addressing physical building performance issues such as energy use, the experiential qualities of buildings, and occupant wellbeing. Each package provided protocols for the field evaluation of existing buildings, activities that contributed to "Building Case Studies" describing student findings. The Resource Packages were designed to be adaptable to the preferences and needs of instructors and the different traditions of particular architecture programs. In 1996 and again in 1998 Vital Signs held case study competitions asking architecture and architectural technology students in the U.S. and Canada to report on a building's physical performance using the program's investigative criteria that required students to document direct, personal experience of buildings. Funding for Vital Signs ended in 1998, but as with many of the initiatives described in this chapter, its resources are still available on the program's website.

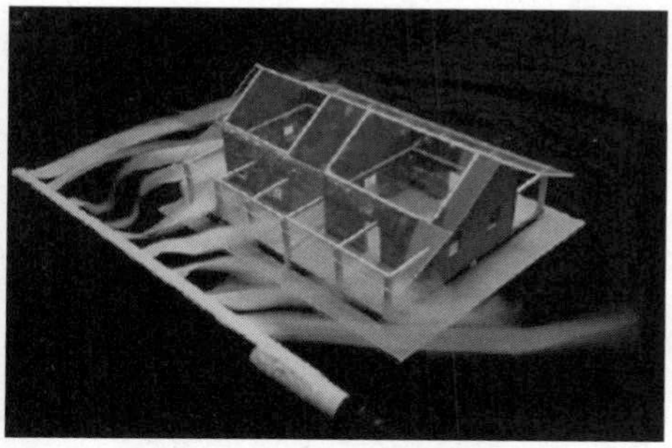

MISSISSIPPI STATE UNIVERSITY

Vital Signs wind simulation shows that a narrow portion of air gets pulled through the dogtrot while the majority goes around the side of the house. (1998)

Back at the University of Oregon, the Spring 1998 issue of Solar Incidents featured a collection of essays on the theme of "Improving Design Education." Within the following years, the Ecological Design Center (EDC) emerged as a student organization combining a conference – H.O.P.E.S.– with the year-long programs of the Solar Information Center. The EDC since became the hub for ideas and innovations in ecological design at the School of A&AA and H.O.P.E.S. has become an annual event, planning its 12th year as this book goes to press.

August 2003
…lis Magazine …es survey of …sign schools

April 2003
…SA Taskforce …ustainability …sts changes …the National …rchitecture …diting Board

2003
Northwest Alliance for Ecological Design Education formed to facilitate exchange between academic and professional groups

November 2003
1st Emerging Green Builders forum conducted at GreenBuild '03

2004
NAAB revised its "Conditions for Accreditation" to include literacy in sustainable design

October 2004
EFS West holds Sustainability & Higher Education Conference

October 2004
Ecotone Publishing launched curriculum expansion project for sustainable design programs

May 2005
1st AIA COTE Ecological Literacy Report grants

October 2005
1st Arizona Symposium on Sustainable Design Education jointly sponsored by the Ecosa Institute & Prescott College

September 2005
ADPSR's New Village Press published *Ecological Design & Building Schools*

April 2006
NW Alliance to release 1st "Northwest Report Card on Ecological Design Education"

2003 **2004** **2005** **2006**

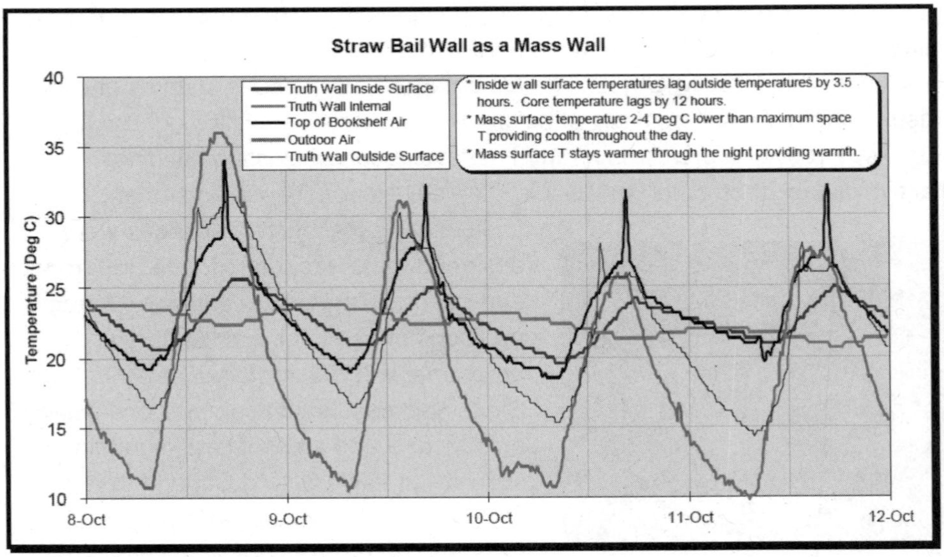

UNIVERSITY OF CALIFORNIA AT BERKELEY / GAIL BRAGER

Students conducted a Vital Signs study of the thermal properties of a straw bale wall by comparing the temperature throughout the wall. (May 1998)

New Participants Join in at the Turn of the Millennium

Beginning in 2000, key organizations previously in the background began to take a leadership role in the ecological design educational arena, including those from the Eastern U.S. and Canada. In June 2000 representatives from various design-related organizations and architecture schools met at the World Resources Institute (WRI) in Washington, DC to discuss sustainability in architectural education. The event was organized by the AIA Committee on the Environment (COTE) and WRI and was reported in *Environmental Building News.*

During the 2000-2001 academic year AIA COTE sponsored a series of articles published in ACSA News, in which notable professors of architecture shared their perspectives on sustainability in design education based largely upon experiences in their own institutions. Unlike other venues for this subject, the ACSA News reached the whole spectrum of architectural faculty rather than exclusively those who had already prioritized teaching ecological design. Reference to the seven articles in this series can be found in this book's Bibliography.

With some time having past since the conclusion of such projects as EASE and Vital Signs, another not-for-profit named Second Nature, dealing with sustainability in higher education, organized a conference at Wingspread in Racine, Wisconsin in August 2001. The conference initially addressed the key question "How Can the Architect Contribute to a Sustainable World?" inspiring a larger look at the role of the architect in society. What fundamentally matters in educating architects? What can we do to inspire and effect architecture education? What is the ecology of architecture? How can the sustainability agenda transform the relationship between the academy and the industry? What does the architect as leader look like? What is the essential role of architects?

From discussions on these questions, guiding principles for a transformed curriculum emerged and strategies were developed to implement sustainability principles in architectural education. The conference is summarized in a Proceedings posted on Second Nature's website. [Glyphis, 2002] Since 2001 Second Nature has explored ways to take its sustainable design education initiative to the next level, however, as with many efforts, theirs required funding to move forward. In 2002, they narrowed their focus to a few high-leverage activities and partnerships for which there was committed philanthropic support, including the Education for Sustainability Western Network (EFS West).

Ever-present during the parade of initiatives having come and gone since its formation, SBSE held its June 2002 annual retreat in Hope Valley, CA, on the theme of "Ecological Literacy: Greening the Architectural Curriculum." To prepare for the retreat, SBSE called for student and faculty contributions of the following.

> 1) Prospects for Ecological Design Education: Insightful essays on ecological design education to frame discussion and developmental work during the retreat. 2) Greening Your Curriculum: Curricular approaches, or specific courses, to be the focus of critique and redesign by retreat participants. 3) Elegant Parts: Effective and engaging tools or class exercises, those that work particularly well at fostering eco-literacy, for a session on teaching methodologies.

Among retreat outcomes, SBSE announced its intention to compile curriculum descriptions contributed by architecture schools into a single accessible location.

Shortly following the SBSE retreat, and after years of joining in with selected U.S. initiatives, Canada held an event all its own. In August 2002, at the Université de Montréal, Professors Ray Cole and Daniel Pearl led a two-day symposium for architecture students, faculty and practitioners from across Canada – "Greening the Curricula: Infusion of Environmental and Sustainability Issues in Canadian Schools of Architecture." A theme among symposium participants, notably more prominent than in much of the U.S. dialog, was the affirmation that Canada support the Kyoto accord and take leadership in environmental responsibility. Gathering multiple institutions for collaboration, idea sharing and awareness of other's curricula was among the main purposes of the 2002 Canadian event. Fostering a pro-active student role was also prioritized.

In April 2003 a Task Force on Sustainability from the Association of Collegiate Schools of Architecture (ACSA) met at their national conferencein

Louisville Kentucky. It was chaired by Kim Tanzer who had monitored the "Greening the Curricula" event. Tanzer communicated a series of Task Force recommendations to the National Architectural Accrediting Board (NAAB) in a memo on "strengthening NAAB criteria to reflect a commitment to the principles of sustainability within architectural curricula." It included specific language on sustainability in the NAAB Student Criteria as well as the addition of the following preamble: "Architects in the 21st century will be expected take a leadership role in stewardship of our global environment. To accomplish this goal students of architecture should find, infused through their education, a philosophy that acknowledges the connected principles of ecology, social justice and economics. This philosophy should be substantiated by providing future architects with the technical knowledge necessary for precise, expert and wise architectural action." [Tanzer, 2003]

Enter on the scene a new player: *Metropolis Magazine*, a periodical that stretches its readers to think outside the box about design and the built environment. From mid-April until early May, 2002, Metropolis conducted an online reader survey about sustainable design in professional practice or educational experience, the results of which were posted to their website. Of the 560 randomly selected respondents, 60 percent responded that they did not receive formal education in sustainability issues, 64 percent that their undergraduate college courses did not cover sustainable design, and 67 percent that their graduate courses did not cover sustainable design.

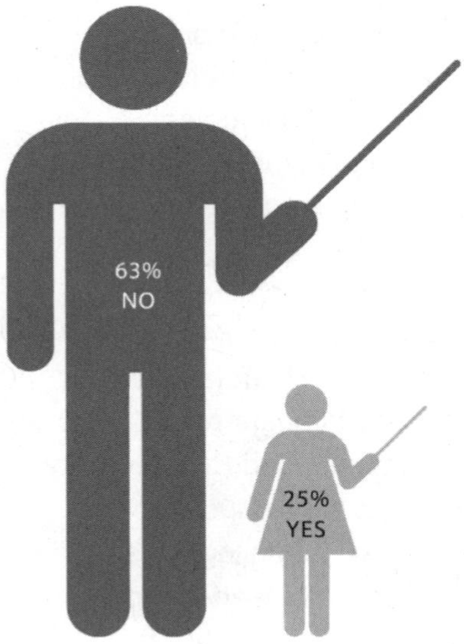

"Metropolis Magazine 2003 Survey: Does your school have a designated faculty advisor on sustainable design? No: 63%; Yes: 25%." Visual courtesy Metropolis Magazine.

A few weeks later, *Metropolis* held a program entitled "Teaching Green" at its annual conference in New York City. From April to May 2003, *Metropolis* conducted a variation on the theme of the previous year's survey. The new online survey invited design educators to participate and gathered 371 responses from deans, department chairs and professors throughout the U.S. and Canada. "[Metropolis] set out to take the pulse of design education in North America, to find out just how well our schools are working sustainability theory and practice into their curricula." The survey results, also posted on the *Metropolis* website, were mixed. Pulling out some of the less impressive statistics, *Metropolis* reported "A mere 14 percent say that their schools are developing programs to educate their teachers about sustainable design. And only 25 percent say their school has a faculty advisor on sustainable design. Is this as alarming to you as it is to us?"

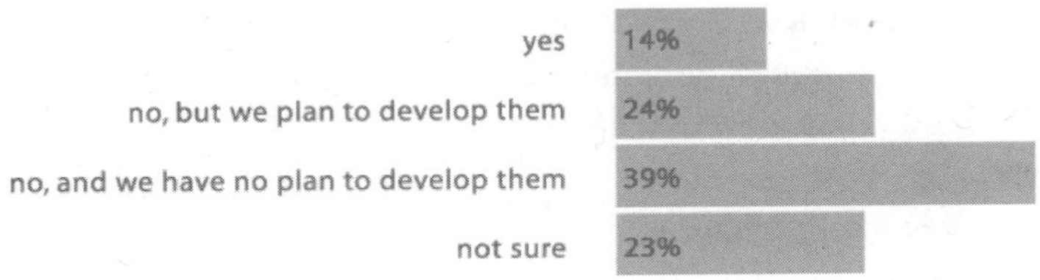

Metropolis Magazine 2003 Survey: "Are you currently developing lifelong learning programs for your faculty in the area of sustainable design?"
Visual courtesy Metropolis Magazine.

The 2003 *Metropolis* survey gained a healthy amount of attention in the field because of its bold tone and challenge to schools not currently focusing on sustainable design education to step up to the plate. Arguably, *Metropolis* presented a glass half-empty perspective, while the contents of this book present a glass half-full. Indeed, this book showcases the exemplary work that is being done in architecture schools and continuing education programs throughout the U.S. and Canada, with the proviso that the examples are only as useful as the replication and innovation that follows them in daily design and building practice.

University-based Educational Research and Development

A recent example of innovative work is Agents of Change, a three-year building-science-oriented project at the University of Oregon supported by the U.S. Department of Education's Fund for the Improvement of Postsecondary Education (FIPSE) from 2002-2005 (some initial funding began in 2000). Under the leadership of Associate Professor Alison Kwok, formerly with the Vital Signs project at U.C. Berkeley, Agents of Charge has trained faculty and teaching assistants from accredited architecture programs to investigate actual buildings, conduct post-occupancy surveys, and develop related exercises to implement at their home institutions. University of Oregon Graduate Teaching Fellows and experienced SBSE faculty lead teams through exercises, protocols, and the case study approach drawn from the Vital Signs Project. Similarly to Vital Signs, Agents of Change provides written customizable "building investigation" exercises with loaner equipment for participants in their training sessions. Program resources are available on its website. Trainings continue to be held for a modest cost in conjunction with selected events held by professional organizations such as the American Solar Energy Society (ASES) and the American Society of Heating Refrigeration and Air-Conditioning Engineers (ASHRAE) Learning Institute.

In Southern California, the California Integrated Waste Management Board (CIWMB) together with the Renewable Energy Institute (REI) at Cal Poly-San Luis Obispo undertook a comprehensive project named Sustainable Environmental Design Education (SEDE) from March 2002 to May 2004. Under the direction of Professor Margot MacDonald, SEDE sought to "improve the adoption of sustainable environmental design principles in higher education and industry continuing education programs in architecture and landscape architecture." SEDE consists of three parts:

1. A survey and needs assessment of sustainable environmental design education in post-secondary architecture and landscape architecture programs throughout North America, with some a emphasis on those in California.
2. A curriculum model for teaching sustainable design to future landscape and architecture professionals that addresses these needs (including references to case studies illustrated above).
3. An outreach strategy to disseminate the model to post-secondary landscape and architecture educators in the State and beyond. [SEDE, 2005]

What specific courses include sustainable environmental design topics at your institution?

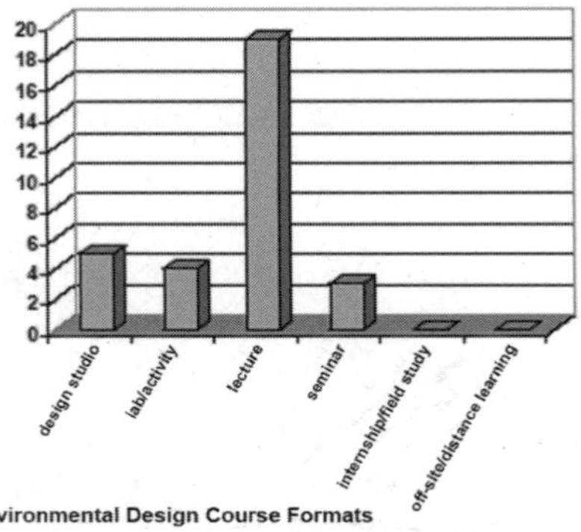

Sustainable Environmental Design Course Formats

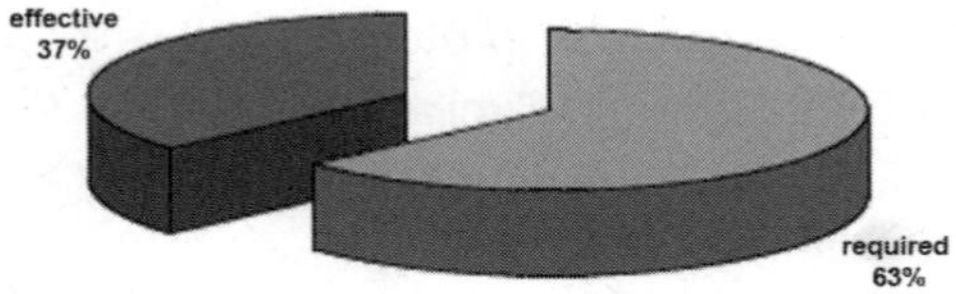

Are faculty interested in teaching sustainable environmental desig at your institution?

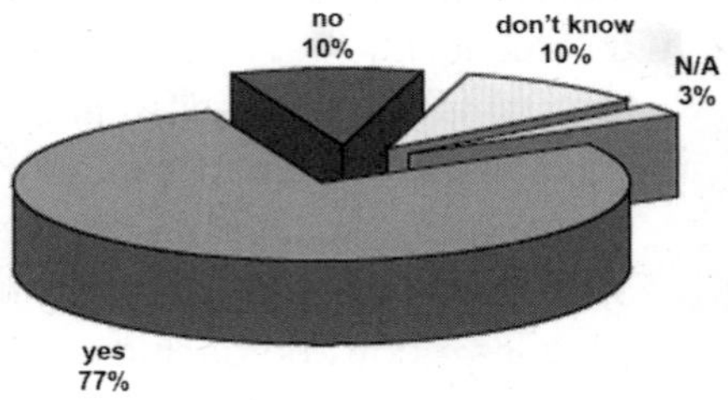

Sample results from SEDE Educator Survey Report (May 200 Visuals copyright California Integrated Waste Management Authority. All rights reserved.

SEDE's detailed materials are available on their well-organized website <www.calpoly.edu/~sede/home>, which includes reports, curriculum models, teaching methods, selected readings and other media, and many other resources for educators. See also the last pages of the Curriculum Resources section of this book for the SEDE proposed Scope of Curriculum.

The results of the SEDE surveys are markedly different in some areas than those of the *Metropolis* survey. For example, 90 percent of SEDE respondents claimed that sustainable environmental design was, in fact, taught at their institutions and 77 percent reported that faculty are interested in teaching sustainable environmental design at their institutions, although a conclusion drawn from the survey is that most of the sustainable design classes are taught by a single instructor.

While different conclusions may be drawn from the data gathered in the SEDE survey compared with the *Metropolis* survey, SEDE has painted the most comprehensive picture to date on the current state of sustainability in architecture education, as well as a singularly comprehensive reporting on landscape architecture education available today.

In addition to the detailed attention paid to surveying current programs, curriculum model development, and resource listings, SEDE's attention to Teaching Methods demonstrates a uniquely deep understanding of the variety of educational formats presented in this book's "Current Educational Offerings" section. SEDE puts forth the notion that "the basis for a sustainable environmental design curriculum incorporates many pedagogical models but in particular should involve place-based, problem-oriented, and participatory learning. Place-based learning demands knowledge of site conditions and their relationship to micro as well as macro scale. This pertains to ecological as well as socio-cultural, economic, and aesthetic conditions. Problem-oriented learning sees the advantage of working with a real, concrete, and complex set of circumstances rather than dealing in a pure, abstract, and simplified world. Participatory learning requires physical and mental immersion in an educational setting of place-based, problem-oriented study." SEDE examines in some detail the various opportunities for ecological design education in such teaching methods as: Experiential Learning; Precedent Studies; Case Studies; Field Trips/Field Studies; Simulations and Role Playing; Internships; and Tools of the Trade. In many ways, these teaching methods mirror the types of "educational structure and setting" research conducted in our own survey leading to the Schools Tables featured later in this book.

Educational Innovation Takes a National Stage

Providing a timely example of the most innovative teaching methods, in October 2002 the first "Solar Decathlon" planted itself on the National Mall in Washington, DC. The program was sponsored by the AIA, the U.S. Department of Energy's Office of Energy Efficiency and Renewable Energy (U.S. DOE EERE) the National Renewable Energy Laboratory (NREL), BP, and the National Association of Home Builders (NAHB). This unique competition called upon teams of architecture and engineering students in participating schools throughout the U.S. to design renewable-energy-powered residential structures that can be erected fully functioning on the National Mall. The teams finance the construction of the super-efficient house through solicited financial donations and in-kind donations of materials and tools. The design must be transportable from its point of origin to Washington, DC while meeting multiple criteria of livability and suitability for performance of household functions for ten days while judges examine, measure and evaluate in competition with other entries. The Solar Decathlon, heralded as a huge success by 2002 participating teams and onlookers, will be repeated in October 2005 with new sets of participating schools, faculty and students.

PHOTO BY WARREN GRETZ, COURTESY OF NREL

Visitors and participants check out the University of Texas at Austin house at the 2002 Solar Decathlon.(September 2002)

Two years after the 2002 "Greening the Curricula" Canadian conference, its organizers held a follow-up symposium, entitled "Greening the Curricula Phase 2: Words to Action". The June 2004 event featured a showcase of student work related to ecological design from across Canada. In an Experimental Green Studio initiative, each school was allowed to explore its own ideas to best incorporate green design principles within the regular design studio context, particularly from the Fall of 2003 through the Spring of 2004. Follow-up includes the publication of a book showcasing the best student work from the Experimental Green Studios with an update on the greening of courses at Canadian schools and a companion website showcasing the best student work and a database for current academic research.

With mounting success and resources, initiatives for ecological design education continue to proliferate, responding to an unprecedented demand for information and understanding of this complex subject. Recently, the U.S. Green Building Council (USGBC) formed an Education Committee that "recommends action items to the USGBC Board of Directors in support of educational programs, college curriculum development, certification programs and outreach.". USGBC also created a virtual chapter named Emerging Green Builders, that promotes leadership among students and young professionals. Recent accomplishments include an Emerging Green Builders forum at the 2003 and 2004 Greenbuild Conferences and a student sustainable design competition.

In 2004 the Environmental Career Center, creators of the National Environmental Employment Report, partnered with the USGBC to disseminate an online “Green Building Survey.” The results of the survey are provided on their website and disseminated in the form of a poster presented at the 2004 Greenbuild Conference in Portland, Oregon. The survey reported that 87 percent of respondents saw an increase in green building industry positions in the coming year. This is good news for emerging professionals hoping to enter this marketplace. The survey represents perhaps the first formal recognition of the design professions as potential environmental careers by an organization that had previously focused on environmental science, law, business, health and almost every discipline except design.

Works in Progress

Back again in the architectural camp, the AIA COTE launched a new initiative in 2005. Made possible by a Tides Foundation grant, “Ecological Literacy in Architectural Education” intended to foster and reward the development of ecological design instructional tools. In a competition closing in February 2005, schools of architecture were asked to submit descriptions for coursework and programs related to sustainability and ecological literacy. Monetary awards of $3,000 were given to one school in each in the following categories: Environmental Foundations in Architecture; Integrated Systems Design; and Sustainable Community Design. Submissions data will be incorporated into an outline of potential education strategies, and selected submissions will be included in a report for general distribution later in 2005.

The USGBC Education Committee has also explored various partnerships and announced in July 2005 that it plans to pilot both an Educational Affiliates and an Educational Partners program later in summer 2005. In the Educational Affiliates program, selected USGBC member companies and organizations will provide introductory LEED trainings through one-hour instructor-led programs, with continuing education credits available. The Educational Partners program is intended to identify and promote partners’ training offerings that serve the broader educational needs of the green building industry.

In the second half of 2004, the National Association of Homebuilders (NAAB) released the latest revision to its “NAAB Conditions for Accreditation,” including, for the first time, a specific mention of sustainable design. This revision responded in part to the request of the ACSA Task Force on Sustainability and to general awareness in the field. The document’s new performance criteria require graduates of accredited programs to have “understanding of the principles of sustainability in making architecture and urban design decisions that conserve natural and built resources, including culturally important buildings and sites, and in the creation of healthful buildings and communities.” [NAAB, 2004] Although this addition represents progress in the way sustainability is framed in the field, in adding the “Sustainable

Design" criterion, the NAAB removed an item from its previous version called "Environmental Conservation: Understanding of the basic principles of ecology and architects' responsibilities with respect to environmental and resource conservation in architecture and urban design." [Malin, 2005] The strength of the new requirement for sustainable design education in accredited architecture programs will be determined over the coming years. As schools document and hopefully go beyond the required instruction in sustainable design fundamentals, their awareness will likely deepen and open to further academic inquiry and application.

In October 2004, Ecotone Publishing Company, a new press dedicated to sustainable design founded by Jason McLennan, launched an independent, interactive three-year curriculum development project in partnership with several design schools. Unlike the various initiatives conducting research via surveys and gathering of curricula, Ecotone is focusing on curriculum development in cooperation with educators and students, with the ultimate goal of producing a textbook, study guide and coursework for ecological design programs and courses throughout the U.S. and Canada. Although acknowledging an abundance of literature on specific aspects of design such as daylighting, materials and energy, Ecotone believes that "without a philosophical basis for these issues it is often not properly understood, or taught. A national dialog on how to 'teach sustainable design' is required." [Ecotone, 2004]

Also in October 2004, Education for Sustainability Western Network (EFS West) held their first "Sustainability in Higher Education Conference" in Portland, Oregon, at which research assistant Megan Clark presented a poster on the subject of this book. Participating in this event was another initiative named the Northwest Alliance for Ecological Design Education, a regional association of students, educators and professionals working to promote and further eco-design education and practice at colleges and universities of the Northwest U.S. The Alliance is planning panels, workshops, conference presentations, an Alliance listserv, curriculum research and promotion, and case studies. They will publish their first annual "Northwest Report Card on Ecological Design Education" in 2006. Meanwhile, Ecosa Institute and Prescott College co-host the first Arizona Symposium on Sustainable Design Education in October 2005, representing the first Southwest U.S. initiative.

This end of the chronological description in this chapter represents merely a slice in time as new ideas and developments in ecological design education continue. Hopefully this compilation serves as both a resource and testimonial to those who have asked themselves "Who's been thinking about sustainability in design education?"

Key Insights into Ecological Design and Building Educational Initiatives

Examination of the initiatives in ecological design and building education described in this chapter reveals a number of important common threads: 1) Architecture schools are central to the broader movement in ecological design education, and to a lesser extent, building education. The initiatives represented in this chapter revolve around formal architectural and environmental design programs provided by higher education institutions. Higher education can serve the development of innovative curricula. Often university-level architecture departments co-exist with related disciplines such as landscape architecture, planning, interior design, historic preservation, and fine arts. Architecture, as an inherently interdisciplinary field of study, tends to not only integrate its related fields and departments but also offer leadership. Not surprisingly, architectural education also provides a proving ground for the ecological design curricula, resources and educational tools developed through outside organizations.

2) When the value of ecological design and building education becomes apparent, everyone tries to get involved. As the intersection of man and nature, ecological design has been at the heart of much activity in the professional world the last several years, yet it took the foresight of several pioneers to begin exploring the integration of ecological design into formal design curricula. These educational leaders saw the most fundamental connection between the processes of making buildings and the processes of working within an environmental context, so formalizing this connection came naturally. Their work was followed and enlarged upon by more and more academic and professional entities, including some whose participation was unexpected. Quite a number of organizations and individuals are involved in the dialog today, and still more are expected in the coming years.

3) Student participation in the development of ecological design and building education is essential. Students are, after all, the consumers of education. They are not just the future of their respective professions, they are education's client. Students bring with them expectations of being changed by the program, and the best programs are also changed by the students. If learning by doing creates a new learning path, so much the better for all involved.

4) Ecological design and building educational initiatives follow the funding. The majority of initiatives represented here were made possible by outside funding. While many worthy programs began with ambitious intentions, the absence of follow-up funding has frequently led to an indefinite pause in the original initiative. At best, this start-and-pause dynamic has resulted in initiatives being applied to actual course offerings or passing to another entity who successfully secured new funding; At worst the result of all the effort invested is obsolescence.

5) Fortunately, the growing body of knowledge in ecological design and building education has proven to be enduring. The Internet has helped prevent the loss of many educational materials developed over the last ten to twenty years. For the modest cost of web-hosting, educational materials can be made accessible to anyone looking for them. This book's appendix, Curriculum Resources, includes websites for several initiatives that have produced or collected ecological design curricula. Each initiative provides a legacy to future innovators by simply remaining online.

6) Follow-up is key to the success of ecological design and building education. The long-term usefulness of discussing, creating and disseminating ecological design educational materials is proven in their regular application in courses and programs and their effectiveness in training people. Students of architecture and related disciplines as well as professionals, are sending an increasingly clear signal that ecological design is what they want to study. While some institutions have been remarkably slow to respond to this call, many others have begun to incorporate ecological design research and pedagogy into their classes. This book's Current Educational Offerings and the appendices, Related Organizations and Individual Instructors, catalog and highlight those institutions, programs and individuals who make this work a reality.

2

Overview of Current Educational Offerings

Growth and Development in Educational Offerings

Thanks to a combination of increased demand and the various educational initiatives described in the previous chapter, one of the primary themes of today is the growth in number and type of educational offerings in ecological design and building. The Schools Directory and Additional Resources sections of this book speak volumes to this point

The geographic spread among today's educational offerings has also increased (see Schools Map, pages 92-93). While students often had to travel great distances to find the courses they sought, today's offerings include more local and regional opportunities spread across North America, with Canada now listing several of its own. In some cases a local or regional green building organization may perform double-duty as the primary educational resource for its geographic area.

While growth in number of programs is a positive trend, development of curriculum depth is at least as important. Many educational programs that were established years ago, including some of those featured in the 1996 version of *Eco-Building Schools*, have expanded their scope. This ongoing development acknowledges the many and varied needs of students while responding to the growing possibilities made available by peer institutions and the industry in general. The Internet has also accelerated awareness of offerings and the sharing of publicly available curricula.

The increased availability and accessibility of green building educational offerings has facilitated greater diversity, rather than homogeneity, in approach. As in any system, diversity yields strength and resilience. In this case it also serves to keep the field challenged and growing. This guidebook illustrates that no single entity has the secret formula for ecological design and building education. Indeed, each student seeks something somewhat unique and personal from his or her educational investment.

Program Educational Content

While this book does not intend to draw hard boundaries among semantic distinctions within this field, some of the larger categories of ecological design and building education merit explanation. This begins with educational content – the substance and scope of educational offerings across varied learning formats.

Natural building & passive heating, cooling and ventilation

First of all, what is natural building? To quote Michael Smith, an established natural building educator: "Natural building is any building system which places the highest value on social and environmental sustainability. It assumes the need to minimize the environmental impact of our housing and other building needs while providing healthy, beautiful, comfortable and spiritually-uplifting homes for everyone. Natural builders emphasize simple, easy-to-learn techniques based on locally-available, renewable resources. These systems rely heavily on human labor and creativity instead of on capital, high technology and specialized skills. . . . [In natural building,] everything depends on local ecology, geology and climate, on the character of the particular building site, and on the needs and personalities of the builders and users. . . . Natural building is personally empowering because it teaches that everyone has or can easily acquire the skills they need to build their own home. . . ." [Kennedy, et. al., 2002]

Depending on the regional context, natural building materials may include any combination of clay or other earthen materials, sand, straw, fieldstone, bamboo, reeds, wood (with emphasis on unfinished and heavy timbers, salvaged logs, and reclaimed wood products). These materials are often combined with salvaged materials such as scrap tires, concrete rubble or containers of various sorts. These materials may form foundations, load-bearing walls, structural frames, roofs, partitions, and finishes.

COURTESY OF YESTERMORROW DESIGN/BUILD SCHO

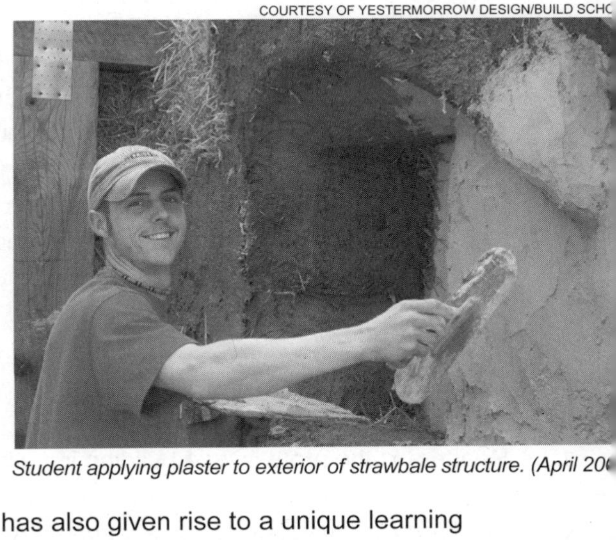

Student applying plaster to exterior of strawbale structure. (April 20

Natural building is taught at schools, centers and informal workshops throughout North America. Individual courses and workshops often focus on one building system, such as wall, framing, roofing or floors, and within that system on one genre, e.g. straw-bale, cob or rammed-earth wall systems. Natural building has also given rise to a unique learning environment, which is a technology exchange gathering often referred to as a Natural Building Colloquium. These colloquia, typically lasting a week, engage several dozen participants at varying levels, allowing students, professionals and international experts the opportunity to explore or refine their skills in roughly a dozen concurrent training and experimental building workshops.

The natural building movement in the U.S. and Canada is a uniquely populist one. It stems from the notion that people everywhere have an inalienable right to sturdy, affordable, healthful housing that they can build themselves. As such, much of the natural building movement works with locally available, renewable resources and generally without patent rights reserved. It stems often from indigenous or traditional building techniques that may be combined with modern, industrial materials and methods. Natural building comes with certain limitations in size and structural loading, though the possibilities are often much greater than imagined and certainly not limited to the single-family dwelling.

Given its inherent qualities, the educational offerings in natural building in the U.S and Canada have typically shared the following characteristics:

- Emphasis on low-impact building materials.
- Orientation to the owner-builder, although professional courses exist as well.
- Major hands-on building component, in additional to theoretical instruction.
- Regional variations depending on local factors such as climate, terrain, and available materials.
- Abundance of warm-weather courses, with fewer offerings in colder months.
- Emphasis on residential design.
- Rural or retreat setting.
- Coupling with passive heating and cooling design strategies

COURTESY OF THE CANELO PROJECT

Athena Steen detailing mortar joints on a dome built out of straw/clay blocks at the S the Children Office location in Ciudad Obregon, Sonora, Mexico. (March 2000)

This last point is an essential one. Passive heating, cooling and ventilation strategies, which experienced a renaissance in the 1970s, still thrive today and have a special connection to natural building. Indeed, the desire for "energy independence" by being "off the grid" is consistent with the use of building materials that rely on renewable resources rather than industrialized products. Natural building and passive design may be seen as a world apart from today's exploding green building marketplace, but the greater truth is that they complement each other in developing sustainable building solutions.

Greener conventional building

Readers in the professional building industry may be more familiar with the ongoing transformation of the market toward greener-than-conventional buildings, products, systems, equipment and operations. According to U.S. EPA-generated definition, "Green or sustainable building is the practice of creating healthier and more resource-efficient models of construction, renovation, operation, maintenance, and demolition." This phenomenon is both policy-driven, thanks to a growing number of local, state and national green building initiatives, and market-driven.

As conventional building is an extremely generalized term, the greener variety begs its own elaboration. Having worked in large professional firms and

PROFILE

Fox Maple — Traditional Building is Natural Building

Fox Maple School of Traditional Building offers hands-on training in traditional timber framing and natural building in a rural Maine setting. Their 40-acre campus features structures built during workshops using traditional methods that together comprise a demonstration learning center that continues to develop. Traditional building is taught at Fox Maple, employing techniques that rely on the natural resources available near the site. Fox Maple's approach to natural building is to wisely use materials that are indigenous or well-adapted to the site and context, while meeting practical contemporary building needs. Fox Maple emphasizes fine craftsmanship and trains lay people and professional builders to become natural building craftspeople. The school's hands-on workshops begin with the construction of a joined timber frame, followed by exploration of natural enclosures such as thatch, straw/clay, wood chip/clay, wattle & daub, cob and straw bales, and are completed by learning finishes of earth plaster. In addition to the variety of short courses taught on the Fox Maple campus, the school offers traveling workshops in such locations as Hawaii and Costa Rica.

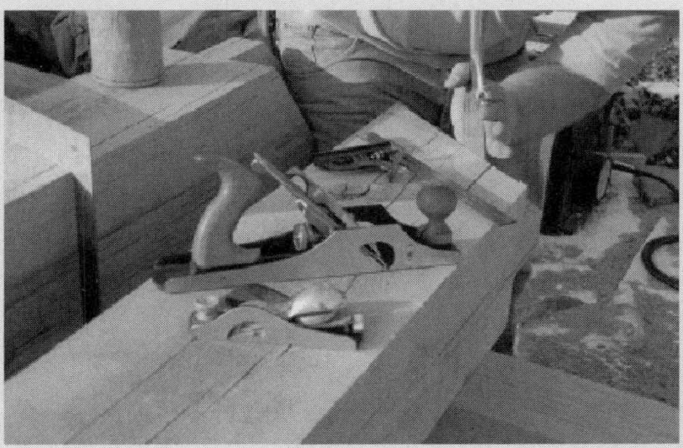

COURTESY OF FOX MAPLE TRADITIONAL BUILDING

Workshop attendees utilize traditional hand tools to shape the framework of a building.

been an active member of the green building movement, I would characterize my field as one that seeks practical alternatives to or improvements upon current practices, including building, site and systems design as well as construction procedures and facility operations. Greener conventional building has rather blurred edges, reaching broadly across the spectrum of low- to high-technology, and addressing building types from single-family homes to the largest commercial facilities. Though usually not as low-impact as the realm of natural building, the sheer magnitude of resource efficiencies multiplied over so many million square feet of buildings, coupled with a high potential for replicability in the mainstream marketplace, lend this emerging field both profound significance and solemn obligation.

Teaching greener conventional building is common in the professional arena and in professional architectural curricula. It generally begins with the thesis that environmental responsibility makes practical business sense. Common areas of instruction include:

- Energy-efficient building envelope design
- Energy-efficient mechanical system design
- Energy-efficient electric lighting design
- Energy simulation and analysis tools
- Daylight design, with simulation and analysis tools
- Water-efficient plumbing systems, including site- and building-water reclamation
- Native and low-maintenance landscape design
- Commercially-available environmentally preferable products, systems and specifications
- Low-emission, low-toxic finish and installation materials

Site & community-scale design

As every building site exists within a context, educational programs often attempt, to varying degrees, to step back and address the surrounding neighborhood, natural environment, or even urban infrastructure. The Shaw EcoVillage EcoDesign Corps in Washington, DC, for example, included a project in which student interns conducted

Photographer: Robert Israel / Ecosa Institute

Students meet with Sim Van der Ryn to review work for the Crossroads Center at Prescott College. (Fall 2001)

PROFILE

Sonoma State Green Building Certification – Professional Development in a University Context

Sonoma State University's School of Extended Education designed this new program with working professionals in mind. This one-year professional development program may be completed over two years. The program is geared toward enabling sustainable building decision-making within a corporate, institutional, non-profit, municipal or individual setting. The program's curriculum incorporates specific assessment criteria such as the LEED® Green Building Rating System, as well as the essential skills of cost-estimating and cost-benefit analysis of sustainable design and technology choices. The program currently consists of six required in-depth courses addressing a variety of subjects, utilizing both classroom and field trip settings. These six courses include: Sustainability and the Built Environment; Site Selection/ Design and Water Efficient Practices; Energy Sources, End Uses and its Impacts; Identifying and Specifying Green Building Materials; Indoor Environmental Quality; and Innovations and Case Studies in Green Buildings. To receive a Certificate of Completion, program graduates must complete an independent green building project, under the guidance of the core faculty. Projects can be done independently or collaboratively with a small team, and community-benefit projects are encouraged. Individual courses are also open to students not enrolled in the full program.

PHOTOGRAPHER: ARMANDO NAVARRO, ASSISTANT DIRECTOR

The Environmental Technology Center at Sonoma State University. (May 2000).

first-person transportation studies of their neighborhood. They timed their trips by bicycle, foot, bus, and car, documenting their analysis and presenting recommendations to the greater community and its decision-makers. College-level courses in site analysis inherently address solar access and air and water flows from beyond a building site, while examining the local conditions of plant species, soil types, and microclimate.

With an admitted emphasis on structures in the built environment, this book does address a range of site-related sustainable design educational issues and offerings. This content includes but is not limited to such topics as:

- Transit-oriented design
- Sustainable community design
- Stormwater management
- Sustainable landscape design
- Permaculture[1]

Response to place is essential to green building. Place-based design has been a consistent theme of several university design departments over the decades. In such programs, vernacular architecture, climatic forces, cultural influences, local ecosystems and materials and global environmental resource issues inform many of the subject-area and studio courses.

Whole-building systems and multi-disciplinary education

While many of the educational offerings included in this book claim to address whole-building or whole-development (building + site) design, this claim, like many in the green building field, should be taken with some skepticism. Its true achievement is challenging to most. A short list of elements common to standard design curricula may include but is not limited to:

- Land use context
- Site analysis
- Site design
- Building massing
- Building structure
- Building envelope
- Passive systems
- Mechanical systems
- Electrical systems
- Plumbing systems
- Indoor environment

1

According to Bill Mollison, the creator of the Permaculture Design Concept, "Permaculture is the conscious design and maintenance of agriculturally productive ecosystems which have the diversity, stability and resilience of natural ecosystems. It is the harmonious integration of landscape and people providing their food, energy, shelter and material and non-material needs in a sustainable way. Permaculture design is a system of assembling conceptual, material and strategic components in a pattern which functions to benefit life in all its forms."

PROFILE

Cal Poly Pomona Center for Regenerative Studies – Sustainable Campus Living

The Center for Regenerative Studies at California State Polytechnic University, Pomona, California grew from concept to reality over the past three decades from the inspiration of landscape architecture professor John T. Lyle. It was renamed the John T. Lyle Center for Regenerative Studies following his death in 1998. Faculty and students live and study together in a dynamic community that makes use of on-site resources, operates with renewable energy, and works with biologically based processes. The highly interdisciplinary educational programs offered by the Center take the form of a new Master of Science in Regenerative Studies, an undergraduate Minor, three courses satisfying Cal Poly's General Education requirements, and an ongoing community workshop series. Subjects covered range from broad overviews of ecological design to specific technologies such as rainwater harvesting and biodiesel fuel. The Center's site, constructed to exemplify the program's concepts, functions as a living laboratory for its own research and educational activities. The 16-acre site is adjacent to the greater Cal Poly campus, and allows students to experience living and working in innovatively designed buildings, while conducting further research and designing new projects. Students completing coursework at the Center, and particularly graduates of its Master of Science Program, develop interdisciplinary systems thinking skills along with in-depth knowledge in their focus areas.

COURTESY OF THE JOHN T. LYLE CENTER

;unspace Residence house for students and interns of the John T. Lyle ɘr for Regenerative Studies at California Polytechnic State University ɔna).

These elements may be taught together as whole systems in introductory design courses, however gaining depth in any one requires specialized focus. In architecture school it is generally expected that studio design courses synthesize subject area knowledge into a well-integrated design process.

Educators committed to a greener curriculum may engage their students in rethinking whole building design, individual components, or some combination of these through an environmental impact lens. Mechanical engineers, for example, may be taught to maximize the use of passive strategies, to design more innovative mechanical systems without passive components, or to simply to specify higher-efficiency conventional equipment. In all cases they would presumably be taught to work in the context of and in concert with other building systems.

Ideally green building education is interdisciplinary, addressing the issues of and interactions among building site, structure, materials, daylight, mechanical, electrical and plumbing systems with appropriately shared emphasis. While this is true of many programs, as represented by the interdisciplinary, integrated studies in this book, it runs against the reality of professional practice that is highly fragmented. Generally speaking, architects do the architecture, engineers the engineering, and so forth, yet a number of current forces are moving this toward better integration. During the past 15 years, there has been a small scale resurgence of the classic designer/builder role. This is especially true in the realm of natural building where architects experimenting with new building systems and materials have involved themselves in the construction process. Within design schools, this dual role is mirrored in design/build studios, such as the Rural Studios program of Auburn University. Furthermore, several innovative institutions have considered interdisciplinary sustainable design certificate programs. Time will tell whether such programs can sufficiently balance generalization with professional focus to provide their graduates smooth transitions into established positions in professional architectural or engineering firms. Fortunately, the field itself is growing more interdisciplinary, as the need for the disciplines to understand each other and foster mutually creative design processes has become common sense, if not thoroughly common practice.

Green building rating systems

As the green building industry strives to better define itself, it has created a variety of rating systems. For the commercial sector, these include the USGBC's LEED (Leadership in Energy and Environmental Design) Green Building Rating System and the U.S. EPA's Energy Star Buildings Program. Residential buildings are currently served by the EPA's Energy Star Homes program as well as local rating systems by such organizations as the Austin Green Builder rating system, Portland General Electric's Earth Advantage

PROFILE

PHOTOGRAPHER: JESSICA ENGLISH

LEED-NC Workshop hosted by the James River chapter of the US Green Building Council. (June 2005)

USGBC LEED Workshops – Coming Soon to Your Neighborhood

The U.S. Green Building Council provides a standardized educational program through its condensed, one-day LEED Training Workshops, Workshops vary in level (Introductory, Intermediate, and Advanced) and content (New Construction & Major Renovations, Existing Building Operations, and Commercial Interiors). In partnership with local green building organizations and educational institutions, the USGBC offers LEED Workshops in dozens of cities throughout the year. LEED Workshops follow the LEED Rating System framework, including Sustainable Sites, Water Efficiency, Energy and Atmosphere, Materials and Resources, and Indoor Environmental Quality. To date, several thousands of individuals have taken this workshop and approximately 20,000 have become LEED-Accredited Professionals, reflecting the Council's uniquely broad-based community of stakeholders, including governmental and not-for-profit entities, developers, design professionals, builders, manufacturers, and other private companies. LEED Workshops are intended both as an entryway into the world of commercial green building and as preparation for the LEED Professional Accreditation Exam which, currently in its second version, has become in many ways more challenging than the first.

PROFILE

SFIA – An Architecture School that Thinks Outside the Box

The San Francisco Institute of Architecture (SFIA) was founded in 1992 by Fred A. Stitt as a school devoted to innovation in design and experimental research and reform in architectural education. Ecological, organic, and unconventional form in architectural design and openness in educational approach are consistant themes across its various programs. SFIA is primarily a graduate school offering both a two-year and a three-year Master of Architecture program, depending on the student's previous degree and experience. It also offers a Master of Ecological Design non-professional degree program, that varies similarly in length and course requirements. SFIA classes are scheduled for evenings or Saturdays, thereby encouraging working professionals and part-time students to enroll. In addition, SFIA offers an Eco Distance Learning program for self-study in Ecological Design, Planning and Construction. SFIA is forming cooperative affiliations with other design schools, such as Merritt College in nearby Oakland, California. Further broadening its reach, SFIA has offered Everything Eco and Eco to Go workshops and has, since 2001, organized an annual national conference – Eco Wave – featuring internationally renowned speakers in ecological design and related fields.

COURTESY OF SAN FRANCISCO INSTITUTE OF ARCHITECTURE

SFIA student design project for Montessori School

PROFILE

Workshop attendees atop an Eco-Dome structure. (2002/2003)

Cal-Earth – Innovative Sustainable Building

The California Institute of Earth Art and Architecture (Cal-Earth) in Hesperia CA has pioneered the concepts of contemporary Earth Art and Ceramic Architecture technologies. Cal-Earth was founded in 1986 by Iranian-American architect and author Nader Khalili, innovator of the Geltaftan Earth-and-Fire System known as Ceramic Houses, and of the Superadobe (earth-bag) construction system. Cal-Earth is dedicated to research and educating the public on environmentally-oriented arts and architecture with an emphasis on appropriate innovation. Their work ranges from technologies published by NASA for lunar base construction to design and development of housing for the world's homeless for the United Nations. Cal-Earth's stated philosophy is based on the equilibrium of the natural elements of earth, water, air, and fire, and their unity in the service of the arts and humanity. Cal-Earth offers an Apprenticeship Program for people who want to learn to build their own home or participate in building a community from earth and the elements. Under the direction of Nader Khalili and English architect Iliona Outram and with the assistant of other experts, Cal Earth employs holistic learning methods. Their Apprenticeship Program addresses individual training needs of each apprentice, balancing design theory and principles taught in conjunction with hands-on experience. In addition to apprentice programs of varying length, Cal-Earth offers three-day intensive workshops and extended workshops of two days per week over four weeks. Cal-Earth also sells Eco-Dome kits including, plans, specifications and calculations for affordable houses using their patented Superadobe Technology, as well as Nader Khalili's books and how-to videos.

Program, Atlanta's EarthCraft House Program, the Scottsdale Green Building Program, and Built Green Colorado, with LEED Homes scheduled for launch in 2005 [all names are trademarks of their owners].

As rating systems generally focus on easily quantifiable criteria and shy away from more complex levels of life-cycle inquiry, their training programs similarly emphasize that which is readily measurable in favor of that which is primarily theoretical. Still, rating systems may serve as educational frameworks when educators seek a convenient, consistently packaged set of learning modules. Because they are proprietary systems, arrangements may have to be made in advance to utilize these systems for education purposes. Most are taught by the authoring organization itself, as in the case of the USGBC's LEED Workshops.

Specific building technologies

Within the context of whole-building/whole-development design, many programs, especially the continuing education or professional development educational programs, offer instruction on specific technologies or systems. On the natural building front, some examples highlighted in the questionnaire we sent to schools to gather data for this book include structural exterior wall systems such as straw-bale, light clay-straw, adobe and cob.

Other areas of ecological design and building education specialization may include the following:

- stormwater management
- daylight design
- green (vegetated) roofing
- passive heating
- passive cooling
- natural ventilation
- energy efficient building envelope
- energy efficient mechanical systems
- solar water heating
- photovoltaic (solar-electric) systems

Courses targeting narrow subject areas such as these are commonly found in continuing education rather than in higher education environments. These focused courses often provide students and professionals with supplementary educational units offered in discreet portions, rather than a full program of study.

Construction processes and building operations

No discussion of green building would be complete without acknowledging the building related issues that occur over time and are process rather than product oriented.

Construction processes that typically create environmental impacts and

PROFILE

Yestermorrow – A Design/Build Emphasis

COURTESY OF YESTERMORROW DESIGN/BUILD SCHOOL

Student marks dimensions on wood framing. (January 2004)

Since 1980, the Yestermorrow Design/Build School in rural Vermont has helped students of varied backgrounds develop critical technical and self-expressive skills using an integrated design/build process that emphasizes sustainable systems and technologies. The well-established Yestermorrow curriculum is structured across three scales of the design/build process: The large scale of Whole Buildings and Communities; the medium scale of Materials, Methods and Building Systems, and the small scale of Architectural Craft and Woodworking. Currently in its 25th year, Yestermorrow offers over 100 hands-on courses annually, ranging from one day to two weeks taught by architects, builders, and craftspeople from across the country. Course levels range from beginner to professional. For its wide-variety of professional-level courses, Continuing Education credits are made available through the American Institute of Architects. While sustainability is respected throughout their entire curricula, it is the major focus of several courses. Twenty four of these courses have become a formal Concentration in Sustainable Design and Construction, offering students the opportunity to explore alternative, innovative, and experimental design and building methodologies and materials. Courses in this concentration currently include such varied subjects as Permaculture design, eco-community planning, earthen construction, landscape design, green remodeling, photovoltaic installation, and deconstruction and materials re-use.

COURTESY OF YESTERMORROW DESIGN/BUILD SCHOOL

Students cutting lumber for wood framing. (June 2004)

offer opportunities for improvement include:
- construction site management
- construction waste creation and management
- construction indoor air quality management

Similarly, building operations that create environmental impacts and offer opportunities for improvement include:
- grounds-keeping materials and practices
- housekeeping materials and practices
- operational waste creation and management
- energy management
- indoor air quality (IAQ) management

COURTESY CARNEGIE MELLON SCHOOL OF ARCHITECTURE

Students bolting loft framing for the Pittsburgh Synergy construction project.

Probably due to their field-based, on-the-job nature, these subjects are rarely taught in the same venues as green building design. They are, however, gaining momentum in the industry through the development of building plan requirements for the subjects listed above. Project teams utilizing the USGBC's LEED Rating System, for example, may earn points toward LEED Certification with plans that include construction waste management, construction IAQ management, or green operations and maintenance. Protection of site water and air quality is required under the LEED system by a prerequisite for erosion and sedimentation control.

Educational Structure & Setting

In addition to the growing richness in course content available today, an aspect which continues to develop is the variety of educational settings and structures. Research in the field of education itself has shown that different styles of teaching may better reach individuals based on their different styles of learning. Some of the most typical educational formats in terms of settings and structures are explored in this book.

Professional and non-professional programs in architecture, architectural studies and related fields generally teach design through a substantial series of courses, extending over a time period ranging anywhere from one to six years, depending on program type. These courses typically begin with the fundamentals of design, structures, building technology, and architectural history and advance through more complex and specialized courses, often allowing for independent study and even foreign study

PROFILE

Ecosa – Alternative Semester Programs Complementing Professional Degrees

The Ecosa Institute in central Arizona was founded in 1996 by English architect/educator Antony Brown. Brown had previously worked on sustainable community concepts as architect in residence at the Cosanti Foundation. Immersed in an ecological matrix, Ecosa's approach emphasizes the responsibility of designers to contribute to a more positive worldview. The school integrates ecological, cultural, historical and aesthetic experience into a rounded design program. Ecosa's mission and philosophy are realized through Sustainable Design semester and summer programs, formally offered since 2000. The fall semester serves students in professional design programs or those with an equivalent background, and emphasizes research and applied design at an advanced level. The spring "pre-design" semester program complements most liberal arts programs and is intended to help students explore a path in the sustainable design field.

Student model of the Prescott College Crossroads Center in Prescott, AZ. (Fall 2000).

Targeted summer programs focus on more specific subjects such as permaculture design and sustainable building materials and methods. In all formats, students live and work together in a collaborative setting, challenging them to solve problems collectively. Throughout the year guest lecturers, including many renowned ecological design experts, provide students direct contact with leaders in the field. Field trips to local Native American sites and other community settings further engage and inspire students' regional sensibilities. Collaboration with local groups allows students to create "real world" solutions that benefit the larger community. Ecosa semester graduates receive a Certificate of Completion in Sustainable Design and in many cases may obtain course credit through their home institution.

opportunities. Architectural education tends to synthesize subject-area coursework into the design studio format, where students are asked, typically individually but sometimes collectively, to address complex problems with design solutions. More and more schools are also incorporating variety and innovation in teaching methods, including design-build programs, semester-long internship programs in local firms, and even experiential learning through alternative, community-based, on-site living programs.

Formal degree programs incorporating ecological design education vary widely, ranging from shorter-term programs devoted to interdisciplinary ecological design studies to longer-term programs that teach ecological design through coursework in environmental control systems, resource-efficient materials and studios that emphasize sustainable solutions. Within academic circles, the debate continues as to the relative merits of developing separate ecological design program tracks versus integrating the material throughout established programs. The latter approach is encouraged by the new NAAB Conditions for Accreditation requirement for Sustainable Design in architectural education. Few schools have made it as central to their mission as Carnegie Mellon's School of Architecture, which offers a variety of professional and post-professional degree programs including a new Master of Science in Sustainable Design.

While professional architectural degree programs most directly prepare students for careers in architectural practice, their required time commitment and focus can be demanding. Interdisciplinary ecological design programs are often more accessible to people in mid-career or those seeking graduate-level education following an unrelated undergraduate track. These alternative offerings are still few and far-between, and include the Sustainable Design Certificate Programs of the Boston Architectural Center and Portland Community College, the San Francisco Institute of Architecture's Master of Ecological Design Program, and Fleming College's new certificate program in Sustainable Building Design and Construction.

More professional development programs

The USGBC's LEED Workshops have led the charge in providing neatly packaged professional green building training to tens of thousands individuals from a wide variety of backgrounds and fields. Meanwhile, other organizations provide professional-level programs that are more specific to their particular audience or field. The Sustainable Buildings Industries Council offers a variety of traveling workshops on such subjects as Designing Low-Energy Buildings and High Performance Schools. Southface in Atlanta offers a Home Energy Rating System (HERS) Training & Certification course. Even real estate professionals now have a course, EcoBroker™, developed just for them.

This type of training, with the many areas it covers, is typically

PROFILE

Fleming College – New Sustainable Building Design and Construction Program

Fleming College in Haliburton, Ontario recently introduced a new certificate program in Sustainable Building Design and Construction. This 20-week intensive is equivalent to a three-semester (45 week) program. The hands-on, practical component of this program involves construction of a sustainable building. The certificate program includes a series of 15 required courses ranging from general subjects such as Contracting and Project Management, Sustainable Building Design, and The Natural, Sustainable and Green Building Movements to specific technical areas such as Exterior Finishes for Sustainable Buildings, Roof Framing and Wall Construction for Sustainable Buildings. Fleming College designed this program for students from diverse backgrounds, including construction industry professionals seeking a specialized skill set, architecture, interior design, or engineering graduates seeking a combination of hands-on and academic ecological design and building instruction, as well as environmental professionals and non-professionals interested in ecological building techniques. The 2005 Sustainable Building project is a new 1800 square foot Haliburton 4C's Food Bank and Lily Ann Thrift Store. Details and photographs of the project can be found on the Sustainable Building Design and Construction program's website.

PHOTOGRAPHER: CHRISTINE JOHNSTON

Students tamping the earthbag foundation for the Haliburton 4C's Food Bank and Lily Ann Thrift Store. (May 2005)

packaged into a single form with variations and condensed into a one-day format as an overview. This educational opportunity is not intended to serve as an in-depth sustainable design education, but rather as a launching pad for further study. Surely anyone interested enough in practicing green building will come from such an introductory workshop with a palette of useful ideas and information to take to the next level.

Finally, while neither manufacturer-driven educational programs nor professional conferences are cataloged in this book, both are common venues for dissemination of useful information to professionals.

Owner-builder formats still thrive

A more environmentally sensitive approach to buildings leads to "conscious" design and building. Consciousness leads to empowerment and designing, building or remodeling one's own home empowers people in their daily lives. As such, the owner-builder course format thrives in green and natural building venues, serving individuals who strive to make environmentally-conscious changes in the pieces of the built environment they personally control. Owner-builder courses tend to share the following characteristics:

- Introductory and advanced courses tailored to the layperson.
- Major hands-on building component, in additional to theoretical instruction.
- Abundance of warm-weather courses, with fewer in colder months.
- Rural, retreat or campus setting, particularly where permanent building projects are undertaken.

COURTESY OF SOLAR ENERGY INTERNATIONAL

Natural Building hands-on workshop attendees stack strawbales to form perimeter walls. (June 2004).

Given the relative simplicity of natural building techniques, compared with the complexity and liabilities of allowing unskilled individuals to use power tools and other dangerous construction equipment, natural building lends itself easily to owner-builder workshops. Straw bale is the most common manifestation of this, offerings hands-on construction opportunities for widely varied skill levels and thus also supporting community-building, often in the form of old-fashioned wall-raisings. Cob, an earthen technique based on the mixture, by foot and hand, of clay, sand, straw or other natural fiber and water, has held particular appeal for women due both to its sculptural qualities and its moderate physical strength requirements.

PROFILE

COURTESY OF THE SOLAR LIVING INSTITUTE

Workshop attendees prepare straw bales for an exterior wall.

Solar Living Institute – For Owner-Builders and Everyone

The Solar Living Institute in Hopland, California began offering workshops in 1992 under its previous identity, the Real Goods Trading Company, a successful retail and catalog supplier of sustainable living products and resources. Spinning-off into a separate not-for-profit educational institution in 1998, the Institute continues to offer a wide range of hands-on workshops in renewable energy, natural building techniques, ecological and energy-efficient design, and sustainable living practices. The Solar Living Institute emphasizes enthusiasm and purposefulness in their approach. They encourage individuals of all backgrounds and skill levels to sample from their extensive menu of hands-on learning opportunities to learn practical techniques for sustainability in their own homes, buildings and lives. Instructors are well-versed in their subjects and students come from across North America and elsewhere. Classes range in length from half-day to five-day and are mostly held on-site at the Solar Living Center, the 5,000 square foot Real Goods demonstration ecological building and 12-acre site in Hopland. A handful of their classes are designed especially for women, and they have also initiated an Urban Sustainability Series on Sunday afternoons in San Francisco. The Solar Living Institute also offers a variety of full-time internship opportunities, that allow interns to live communally on-site and support the activities of the Institute and the Solar living Center. Interns are eligible to attend workshops free of charge on a space-available basis.

Owner-builder courses tend to be offered by small organizations or through continuing education departments of community colleges. The Building Education Center in Berkeley, California, for example, features intensive home design courses as well as short courses in such varied subjects as Carpentry Basics for Everyone, Ceramic Tile Installation, Interior Plastering, Bamboo Building and Architectural Sketching. The courses are designed to provide its students a customized set of skills they can use in their own small-scale building projects.

Professional building courses appearing on the scene

An increasing number of professional construction programs in ecological building exist today, many of which share some, if not all, of the attributes of owner-builder programs, but are geared toward development of marketable skills. The newly established Green Advantage program, being piloted in southeastern states, is tailored more to the needs of builders and subcontractors. A new program at Laney Community College in Oakland, California has students in its Carpentry Department work on affordable housing projects using environmentally-friendly building techniques (Laney's GreenBuilt Housing Project). Similarly, Southface in Atlanta offers courses in homebuilding that conform to Atlanta's EarthCraft House rating system, while the Yestermorrow Design Build School in rural Vermont offers a varied professional curriculum that complements its home design/build curriculum.

Natural building organizations also offer professionally-oriented trainings in specific techniques, geared toward those who seek a career in natural building or to supplement their building skills. Such training is currently available through the California Straw Building Association, Cob Cottage Company's North American School of Natural Building, the Island School of Building Arts, Rocky Mountain Workshops, and the Timber Framers Guild, among others.

More online content and self-study opportunities

At the other end of the technology spectrum, a few organizations have taken advantage of teaching possibilities afforded by the Internet. Solar Energy International, for example, offers Photovoltaic Design and Solar Home Design courses online so that its students need not travel to Colorado to take advantage of this portion of its offerings.

Other organizations such as the San Francisco Institute of Architecture (SFIA) and the International Institute for Bau-biologie and Ecology, Inc. (IBE) include, in their programs, correspondence courses with some online

PROFILE

Solar Energy International – Taking Energy Education to the Internet

Like many other schools featured in this book, Solar Energy International (SEI) SEI offers a broad-range of hands-on workshops, mostly week-end and week-long in length. These workshops cover over 20 specific subjects in the topic categories of Solar Electricity, Wind Power, Micro-hydro, Solar Home Design & Natural House Building, Solar Thermal, Renewable Fuels, Women's skills and other topics. Based in Carbondale, Colorado, SEI is able to offer these workshops in eleven locations in the U.S., Canada, Nicaragua and Cost Rica, through partnerships with other organizations. To further extend its reach across the globe, SEI began offering two of its courses, Photovoltaic Design and Solar Home Design in unique online course formats. The online courses are offered multiple times per year, and the Photovoltaic Design course provides 60 cumulative hours of training, that may be used toward professional certification. After completing the distance course, students may choose to attend related hands-on workshops for a reduced fee.

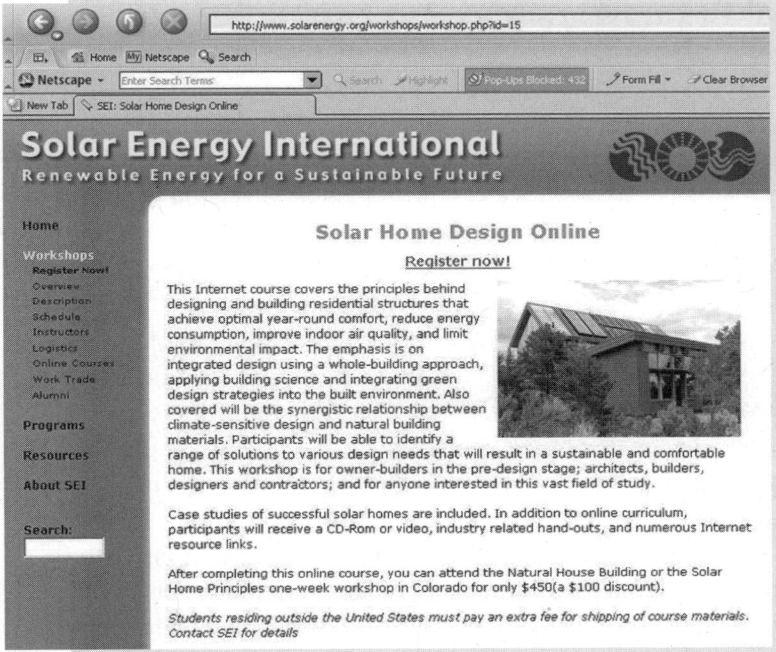

COURTESY OF SOLAR ENERGY INTERNATIONAL

This Solar Home Design workshop is one of two online programs offered by Solar Energy International. (June 2005).

components. SFIA's program is marketed as "Eco-Distance Learning," each course requiring an average of 36 hours of study and providing 3 units of academic credit toward an Associates Degree and Technical Certification Program, a Bachelor of Science in Ecological Design degree, or a Master of Ecological Design degree.

RedVector.com, an exclusively online educator for engineering, design and construction professionals, currently offers 20 continuing education courses for architects in the category of Sustainable/Green Design. Their short read-and-quiz courses are based on chapters from textbooks, such as Alternative Construction: Contemporary Natural Building Methods.

Service learning and community building

In a select few recent programs, a service-learning format is the primary educational vehicle. In the EcoDesign Corps of the Shaw EcoVillage Project, high school students enrolled in paid internships learn how to identify important issues in their communities and to address those issues through hands-on action projects. Meanwhile, Auburn University's Rural Studio, keeping the legacy of the late Samuel Mockbee alive, operates on the principle of "context-based learning," wherein students take up residency in poverty-stricken Hale County, Alabama to design and build housing for an actual client in need.

Organizational Framework and Projects

An interesting related issue is that of the organizational identity and structure of the various schools themselves. The term "school" is applied broadly in this book, including such entities that may be best described as "educational centers." Research centers within universities and various organization types outside of the university environment abound in the field of ecological design.

Often organizations that feature research as part of their mission also provide educational programs to disseminate their research. Examples include the Florida Solar Energy Center, the Energy Center of Wisconsin, Southface Energy Institute in Atlanta and the Lighting Design Lab in cities of the Pacific Northwest. Similarly to local and regional green building programs, these organizations often serve as local hubs for ecological design and building activity. They host events, co-sponsor programs with related organizations, make books and material sample libraries available to the public, and sometimes even create demonstration buildings to house their operations. The Center for Maximum Potential Building Systems, a research organization in Austin Texas, whose primarily educational mechanism is its ongoing internship program, has built experimental structures on its grounds to demonstrate a variety of low-impact building techniques. Tours of the built projects provide educational outreach to the public.

PROFILE

Auburn Rural Studio – Service-Learning

The Rural Studio at Auburn University's School of Architecture was founded in 1993 by two professors, Dennis K. Ruth and the late Samuel Mockbee. Their concept for the Studio was to provide a hands-on, interactive means for training students in the art of building their own designs using resource-efficient and innovative technologies, while improving living conditions in rural Alabama. Rural Studio's mission is to allow students to put their education and values to work as citizens of a community. The program utilizes a model of "context-based learning," in which Rural Studio students "refine their social conscience" by taking up residency in Hale County, Alabama to "share the sweat" with housing clients who live far below the poverty level. This service-learning program partners with the state and local welfare agencies to provide suitable and dignified housing and public gathering places. In collaboration with the project's practicing architect, student residents have designed and built seven houses and numerous community projects such as a children's center, playground, public pavilions, a senior center and amphitheatre. Students are immersed in the social, cultural and technological facets of the building process, and learn critical planning, design, and building skills while developing leadership qualities. The students also experiment with unconventional materials, methods, and building technologies that may be replicated for wide-spread implementation. The Rural Studio consists of three programs, one residency program each for second year and thesis year Auburn University students, and a third for non Auburn University graduate students who work both on a joint project and individual community outreach projects in their own discipline.

COPYRIGHT 2000, TIMOTHY HURSLEY

d Mrs. Harris enjoy the sunset on the porch of their home, designed ıilt by students of the Rural Studio.

While many educational organizations have not-for-profit status, this is not a universal characteristic, particularly when the educational component is mixed with other professional activities such as design, consulting, construction or other technical services. Furthermore, some schools and educational centers use book and journal publishing as an alternate means of sharing their experience in the field. For example, Rob Roy of the Earthwood Building School has written at least seven books and created at least five videos on cordwood masonry construction and related subjects. Other organizations focus on regular newsletter publications to provide ongoing information sharing – these publications are included for each school listed in the Schools Directory section of this book.

PHOTOGRAPHER: ROB ROY

Earthwood Building School campus, West Chazy, New York.

Finally, schools and educational centers may play a unique role in their local community. In addition to hosting lectures, workshops, or conferences, some educational centers make other types of programs possible, as well. Arcosanti has a large enough space to host occasional concerts, while the Solar Living Institute, founded in relation to the Real Goods retail store in Hopland, California, hosts an annual “Sol Fest” renewable energy and sustainable living fair, which has been attended by 4,000 to 10,000 people annually the past six years, exposing the general public to sustainable technologies, resources, products and well-known speakers in the field.

Career Potential

While prospective ecological design and building students seek general understanding from their education, an increasing number are determined to make a career out of it. Eighty seven percent of participants in a 2004 Green Building Survey, conducted by the Environmental Career Center, saw an increase in green building industry positions in the coming year. And the types of positions in this field are as diverse as the educational opportunities leading to them.

While the path from professional architectural education to its corresponding career track is quite well supported in the industry itself, specializations in green building are throwing in an interesting twist. Ecological design and building is at once a broad-based and highly interdisciplinary

PROFILE

Earthbag construction at Ecovillage Training Center. (2004)

COURTESY ECOVILLAGE TRAINING CENTER

Ecovillage Training Center at The Farm – Ecological Education in an Ecovillage Context

The Farm is an intentional community in rural Summertown, Tennessee originally founded in 1971 as a communal economy with a blend of traditional and non-traditional cultural values. In the early 1990s, The Farm began a process of redefining itself as an Ecovillage, prioritizing ecological sustainability in all of its expression. Today The Farm plays a key role in the Global Ecovillage Network, that includes intentional communities from around the world, both rural and urban. In 1994, equipped with charitable sponsorship and a targeted mission, The Farm established an Ecovillage Training Center. Today it offers courses ranging from weekend workshops to month-long Ecovillage Apprenticeships, all emphasizing ecologically-efficient technology, land management and master planning in the context of an intentional community. The on-site residential Ecovillage Apprenticeship programs focus on natural building, Permaculture, and organic food production. Acceptance into the apprenticeship program is highly competitive: only 15 to 20 out of 400 to 500 applicants are accepted each year. Ecovillage Apprentices at The Farm learn ecology, energy and resource conservation, social and community skills, and the economics of sustainability through study, hands-on work, guest lecturers and field trips. College credit for this program may be granted at the discretion of the student's home university.

background to develop, yet it is seen by much of the conventional building industry as specialty. Design firms may hire green building consultants, and they may also create in-house positions for those professionals who focus their efforts on more environmentally sound options to conventional practice.

Professionals in ecological design and building may themselves focus in any number of primary subjects such as resource-efficient materials, stormwater management, indoor air quality, natural building design and construction, daylighting or energy efficient design and engineering. Consultants in ecological design and building are engaged in alternative careers, that is, they are playing a professional role other than direct responsibility for design or construction. Such alternative careers may also take the form of advocacy, research, planning, or public policy.

As the demand for green building grows throughout North America, professionals with skills and experience in any or all of these areas will find their expertise in ever-increasing demand. This is further enhanced by the rising demand for LEED rating system expertise. It should be noted, however, that a focus on strategies for achieving LEED credit points, rather than prioritizing sustainability of the whole is a potential pitfall of this system.

Ecological design and building education offers the opportunity for exceptionally valuable and meaningful study, and many former students have already applied their education to rewarding careers that benefit society, the environment, and the economy. The door is indeed wide-open. Students today have been given many gifts by the growing green building industry, including the inspiration of role models who repeatedly demonstrate there are always new routes to successfully enter the field.

PHOTOGRAPHER: ROBERT ISRAEL / ECOSA INSTITUTE

Students engage in discussion with Paolo Soleri at the Cosanti Foundation in Scottsdale, Arizona. (Fall 2001).

PROFILE

Carnegie Mellon – Masters of Science in Sustainable Design

Carnegie Mellon University asserts that they have identified sustainable design as central to the mission of the School of Architecture. Beginning with the 2002-2003 academic year, Carnegie Mellon began offering the first Master of Science degree program in Sustainable Design. Their 9-month and 16-month graduate programs are intended for graduates with architecture related and interdisciplinary backgrounds, and allows admission with advanced standing in certain cases. The program is structured to prepare design professionals for careers in sustainable design and high-performance green building. Among key focus areas currently offered or under development, are those of building systems integration and occupant well-being, that relate to the work of The Center for Building Performance and Diagnostics (CBPD), a National Science Foundation Industry/ University/ Government Cooperative Research Center, operating within CMU's School of Architecture. Carnegie Mellon's commitment to Sustainable Design is also exemplified through its existing undergraduate professional architecture program, which features 5 studios and 9 required courses where environmental quality is central, along with 3-5 departmental electives in addition to 8-12 university electives in the area of sustainability. Presently, four full-time faculty and six adjunct faculty consider design for sustainability central to their teaching, research and/or practice, and work in sustainability both on campus and locally in cooperation with Pittsburgh's Green Building Alliance.

PHOTOGRAPHER: STEPHEN LEE

Students from the Pittsburgh Synergy group construct the framing for their entry into the 2005 Solar Decathlon. (June 2005).

PROFILE

University of British Columbia – Integrated Sustainability, both Curriculum and Campus

The University of British Columbia (UBC) in Vancouver has made its commitment to sustainability known across department lines. The School of Architecture offers, under the heading of Environmental Studies, five ecological design and building science courses. These include fundamental courses in Environmental Systems and Controls and advanced courses in Context to Green Design; Light, Colour and Space; and Energy, Building and Environment. Degree programs in this school are structured both as professional and non-professional tracks including the Master of Architecture, Master of Advanced Studies in Architecture and Environmental Design programs. UBC architecture professors, most notably Ray Cole, have long demonstrated leadership in the Canadian green building movement and in the advancement of sustainable design education in Canadian schools of architecture. UBC's C.K. Choi Building for the Institute of Asian Research distinguished itself as one of landmark buildings of the contemporary commercial green building movement in 1996, followed by the Liu Centre for the Study of Global Issues in 2000 and other campus green building projects in progress. UBC's Campus Sustainability Office works internally to move toward sustainability in all of its operations and capital projects, while their Institute for Resources, Environment and Sustainability, established in 2002, brings different disciplines together to promote research and implementation of sustainable development in the broader community.

PHOTOGRAPHER: NIGEL REEVES

Students outside one of UBC's award-winning green buildings, the C.K. Choi Building. (2004)

PROFILE

Green Advantage® – A Program Just for Builders

Green Advantage is an environmental training and certification program crafted specifically for building-related practitioners, primarily contractors, sub-contractors and trades people. Modeled in part on the USGBC's LEED training and accreditation programs, Green Advantage has tailored its approach to the actual building and construction management processes. Green Advantage certified building professionals demonstrate knowledge to home buyers and other clients about green building techniques and approaches. Their training focuses on the areas of sustainable land planning, development and management; energy- and water-efficient building technologies; disaster- and pest-resistant sustainable construction technologies; indoor air quality and healthy construction. Though based in Virginia, Green Advantage began by piloting programs in Florida and Colorado, for which certified professionals are currently listed on their website. Officially recognized as a USGBC Educational Partner, Green Advantage is currently developing relationships with USGBC chapters across the U.S. to build future program extensions on a national scale.

PROFILE

Building Education Center – Focus on the Owner-Builder

The Building Education Center in Berkeley, California is a not-for-profit educational organization offering a comprehensive menu of educational programs designed for the owner-builder at different skill levels. In additional, some advanced courses are geared to developing marketable professional skills. Course formats include half-day short courses, one-day seminars and hands-on workshops, and intensive courses of varying length. Many offerings in each of these categories include an emphasis on ecological design and building techniques, including Residential Green Building and Remodeling, Solar Electricity for Your Home, and Alternative Materials Cob and Strawbale. In addition to their 60+ courses, the Building Education Center offers an ongoing series of free lectures to the Bay Area community and sells a selected list of useful reference books.

COURTESY BERKELEY EDUCATION CENTER

Paul Hara measuring roof frame at Berkeley Education Center, (2005)

3

Schools Directory and Program Tables

- Methodology
- School Program Tables
- Schools Map
- Schools Directory

Methodology

This explanation of methodology describes the process and criteria for compiling the following directory. In the summer of 2003 intern Eli Zigas joined me in rethinking the original 1995 questionnaire I had used to assemble my 1996 directory. The current status of the schools listed in that directory was reviewed, and the list greatly expanded, adding professional continuing education and Canadian resources to the scope. Initial questionnaires were sent in July 2003, while a database was built to house the responses. In early 2004, then joined by research assistant Megan Clark, the effort was renewed with a revised version of the questionnaire and a target of higher education programs including architecture and related programs.

In total, over 100 questionnaires were sent between mid-2003 and early 2005 to a variety of non-professional continuing education programs, professional continuing education programs, and formal architecture and design schools. Of these, over 90 responses were received, some of which led to a re-categorizing from a "school" to a "related organization." The 82 institutions or programs presented as "schools" in the Directory include 68 for which questionnaires were received, and 14 for which questionnaires were not received. Schools that had previously completed a 2003 questionnaire received a 2004 questionnaire update to complete for consistent data gathering. A section was also provided in the questionnaire for up to three recommendations of other schools or programs to contact, reflecting another effort to be inclusive in the scope of the research.

The main information requested in the questionnaires was presented under three overall categories of "Program Content," "Educational Structure and Setting," and "Organizational Framework and Projects" – an attempt to gather program information about What, How, and By Whom, emphasizing the types of information potential students would find useful in making a program selection. The headings of the columns presented in the School Program Tables that follow are identical to those listed on the 2004 version of the questionnaire, which asked the respondent to simply indicate Major, Minor, or Not Applicable for each item. The information presented in these tables includes only those 68 schools from which questionnaires were received, while all 82 schools are listed in the Schools Directory at the end of this section. Program narratives listed in the directory are lightly edited versions of those provided by the schools themselves. Where no questionnaire was received, I drafted a brief description drawn from publicly available information.

Ecological Design and Building Schools applies the term "school" in a manner that is intentionally broad, but not without limits. In order to be listed as a "school" in this book, the institution had to have an ecological design and/or building educational program offered on a continual basis, with more than one instructor, more than one course offering and/or internship program, and a physical location where activities were held or headquartered. Ecological design and building institutions meeting some but not all of these criteria were often listed in the Additional Resources chapter under Related Organizations or Individual Instructors. Furthermore, although commercial product and equipment manufacturers often provide trainings to professionals on the environmental benefits of their goods, these manufacturer-based programs were not included in order to limit the scope to more objective educational offerings.

The rationale in this approach was to limit the survey to those schools that had demonstrated substantial ecological design content and to minimize the possibility of misrepresenting programs with minor or inconsistent ecological design offerings as leaders in the field. While I acknowledge that there may be cases where schools with emerging ecological design and building programs appear to be "left out" of the survey, it is my desire that this guide provide incentive for further program development so that the list of showcased schools will grow in the coming years.

Terms and Definitions

The pages that follow include three different formats presenting this book's listings of Schools:

School Program Tables

Responses from 68 schools are incorporated into matrices that reflect their course content and organizational structure. In an attempt to provide more targeted information to the variety of readers, schools are divided among three major categories, as described below, and alphabetized by name. In cases where a school fits more than one description, the category that reflects the majority of the school's activities and educational offerings is used.

Continuing Education – Non-Professional
The Non-Professional Continuing Education category includes programs that offer ecological design and building courses for general and non-professional application, that offer the majority of their courses to anyone, regardless of background, and/or that offer primarily non-professional internships in ecological design and building.

Continuing Education – Professional
The Professional Continuing Education category includes programs that offer ecological design and building courses for professional application, including advanced professional training, that offer courses for that assume prior professional education, and/or that offer some form of professional certification.

Higher Education
The Higher Education category includes postsecondary educational institutions that offer professional and/or non-professional degree programs in architecture, design and building technology with an emphasis in sustainable design, and/or programs as defined above with access to university research centers focused on sustainable principles.

All school listings have an ecological design and/or building educational program offered on a continual basis, with more than one instructor, more than one course offering and/or internship program and a physical location where activities are held or headquartered. Ecological design and building entities meeting some but not all of these criteria are listed alphabetically by state and province in this book's Additional Resources chapter under "Related Organizations" or "Individual Instructors." Additional Resources also includes "Curriculum Resources" alphabetized by name.

Schools Map

Locations of all schools solicited for questionnaires are marked by a number corresponding to the city name, which appear alphabetized by state and province. Note that in the instance when two schools exist in the same city it has only been recorded once.

Schools Directory

Contact information and brief program descriptions for 82 schools are alphabetized by state and province, reflecting the larger pool from which questionnaires were solicited. The icons accompanying each entry correspond to the three categories above, as well as a fourth, "Hands-On" which is used to denote schools that offer hands-on building courses.

....

A master "Index of Lisitings" for Schools, Curriculum Resources, Related Organizations, and Individual Instructors, alphabetized by name and indicating both location and major category, can be found at the back of this book.

Highlights of the Ecological Design and Building Schools questionnaire responses

Detailed questionnaire responses for 68 schools are displayed in the pages that follow. But first, a few highlights from each of our three major schools categories:

Questionnaire Highlights: Continuing Education - Non-Professional

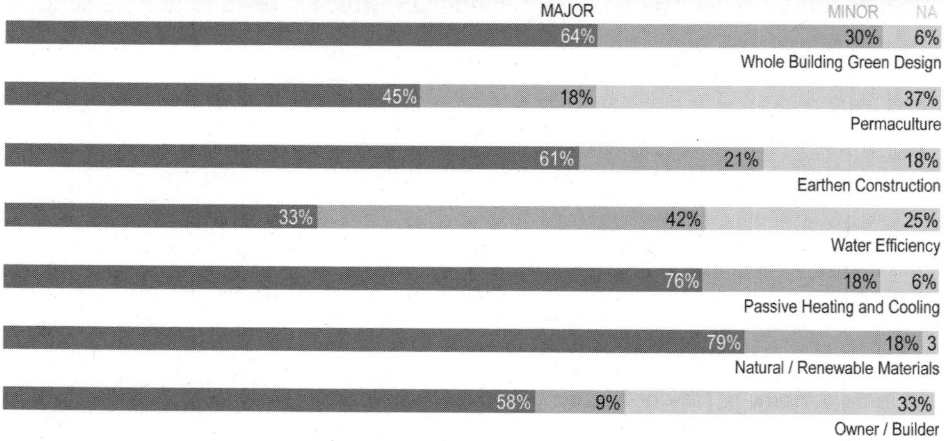

Questionnaire Highlights: Continuing Education - Professional

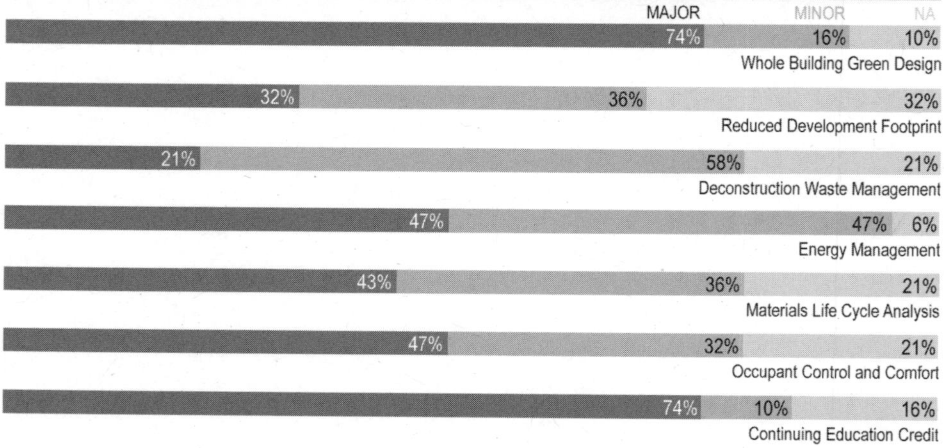

Questionnaire Highlights: Higher Education

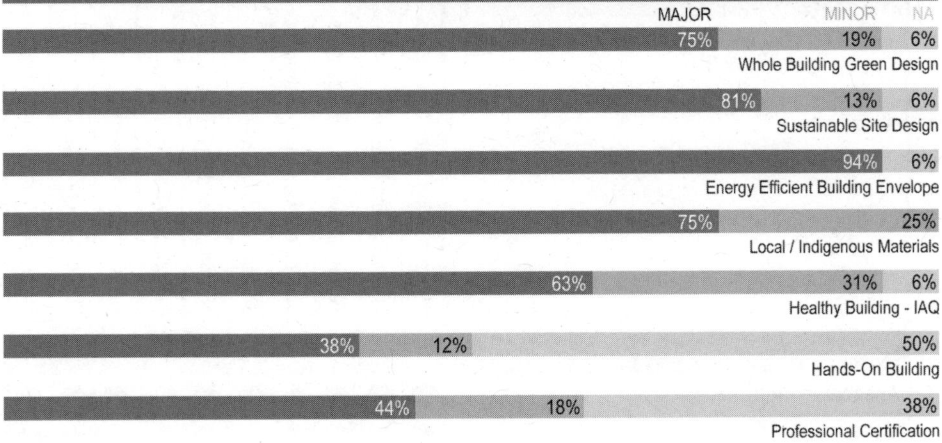

KEY

- ● Major Aspect
- ◓ Minor Aspect
- ⊗ Not Applicable

Continuing Education - Non-Professional	General Green Building									
	Whole Building Green Design	Green Building Rating	Residential Design / Construction	Commercial Design / Construction	Building Reuse / Renovation	Affordable Building / Housing	Participatory Design Process	Transit-Oriented Design	Reduced Development Footprint	Sustainable Community Design
Apeiron Institute	●	◓	●	●	●	●	●	●	●	●
Aprovecho Research Center	●	⊗	⊗	◓	⊗	◓	◓	⊗	◓	●
Arcosanti	⊗	⊗	●	●	◓	◓	◓	●	●	●
Building Education Center	◓	⊗	●	⊗	●	●	●	◓	◓	⊗
Cal-Earth Institute / Geltaftan Foundation	●	⊗	●	◓	⊗	●	●	◓	●	●
Canelo Project	◓	⊗	●	◓	◓	●	●	◓	◓	◓
Center for Maximum Potential Building Systems	●	●	◓	◓	◓	●	●	◓	●	●
Cob Cottage Company	●	⊗	●	◓	⊗	●	●	●	●	⊗
Cobworks	◓	⊗	●	⊗	◓	●	●	⊗	◓	◓
DAWN Southwest	◓	⊗	⊗	⊗	◓	●	◓	⊗	●	●
Earthwood Building School	●	⊗	●	◓	⊗	●	◓	⊗	●	⊗
EcoVersity	●	⊗	●	⊗	●	●	●	⊗	●	●
Eco-Village Training Center	●	⊗	⊗	⊗	⊗	⊗	⊗	⊗	⊗	●
Everdale Environmental Learning Centre	●	◓	●	⊗	◓	◓	●	⊗	◓	⊗
Goshen Timber Frames	◓	◓	●	◓	●	●	●	⊗	⊗	⊗
Groundworks	●	⊗	●	⊗	◓	●	●	⊗	⊗	⊗
Heartwood School for Homebuilding Crafts	●	⊗	●	⊗	⊗	●	●	⊗	◓	◓
House Alive	⊗	⊗	⊗	⊗	◓	◓	⊗	⊗	◓	⊗
Joslyn Castle Institute	●	●	⊗	⊗	●	●	●	●	●	●
Kortright Centre	●	⊗	⊗	⊗	⊗	⊗	⊗	⊗	⊗	⊗
Kūpono Natural Builders	●	⊗	●	⊗	⊗	●	●	⊗	◓	◓
Montgomery College	●	●	●	●	⊗	⊗	⊗	⊗	⊗	⊗
Occidental Arts & Ecology Center	◓	⊗	◓	⊗	⊗	⊗	◓	⊗	◓	●
O.U.R. Ecovillage	●	◓	●	⊗	●	●	●	⊗	●	●
Pangea Partnership	●	◓	●	◓	●	●	●	⊗	●	●
Rocky Mountain Workshops	◓	⊗	●	●	⊗	◓	◓	◓	◓	⊗
Seven Generations Natural Builders	●	◓	●	◓	◓	●	●	⊗	◓	⊗

Sustainable Site Design	Stormwater Managment	Sustainable Landscaping	Permaculture	Green / Vegetated Roofing	Exterior Lighting	Dome Building	Earth Sheltering	Earthen Construction	Masonry Construction	Straw-based Construction	Timber Framing	Non-Timber-Framed Wood Construction	Site Protection / Reduced Disturbance	Deconstruction Waste Management	Construction Waste Recycling	IAQ Management	Water Efficiency	Innovative Wastewater Treatment	Energy Efficient Building Envelope
Sustainable Sites						Construction Method							Management						
●	⊗	●	●	◓	◓	⊗	◓	◓	◓	●	◓	●	◓	●	●	◓	◓	●	●
●	◓	●	●	⊗	◓	⊗	⊗	◓	⊗	●	●	⊗	◓	⊗	⊗	⊗	◓	◓	●
●	◓	●	●	◓	◓	⊗	◓	◓	●	◓	◓	⊗	⊗	◓	◓	⊗	◓	◓	●
⊗	⊗	⊗	⊗	⊗	⊗	⊗	⊗	⊗	⊗	●	●	●	◓	◓	◓	⊗	⊗	◓	◓
●	◓	◓	◓	◓	◓	●	●	●	●	◓	⊗	⊗	●	◓	◓	◓	◓	◓	●
●	⊗	●	◓	◓	●	◓	◓	●	◓	●	◓	◓	◓	⊗	⊗	⊗	◓	⊗	●
●	●	●	●	◓	◓	⊗	⊗	●	◓	●	●	⊗	●	●	●	●	●	●	◓
●	◓	◓	◓	●	⊗	⊗	◓	●	●	●	●	●	◓	◓	◓	◓	◓	◓	●
●	⊗	◓	◓	◓	⊗	⊗	●	●	⊗	◓	●	●	◓	◓	●	◓	◓	◓	◓
●	◓	●	●	⊗	⊗	●	●	●	●	●	●	●	●	●	●	●	●	●	●
⊗	◓	⊗	⊗	●	⊗	⊗	●	⊗	●	⊗	◓	◓	●	◓	◓	⊗	⊗	⊗	●
●	●	●	●	⊗	⊗	●	●	●	⊗	●	⊗	⊗	●	●	●	●	●	●	●
●	●	●	●	●	●	●	⊗	●	⊗	●	⊗	⊗	⊗	⊗	⊗	⊗	●	●	⊗
●	◓	⊗	●	◓	⊗	⊗	⊗	⊗	⊗	●	⊗	⊗	◓	◓	◓	⊗	●	●	●
⊗	⊗	⊗	⊗	⊗	⊗	⊗	⊗	⊗	⊗	⊗	●	●	⊗	⊗	⊗	⊗	⊗	⊗	●
⊗	⊗	◓	●	⊗	⊗	◓	⊗	●	●	⊗	◓	⊗	●	●	●	⊗	⊗	◓	⊗
◓	⊗	⊗	⊗	⊗	⊗	⊗	⊗	◓	◓	⊗	●	●	◓	◓	◓	⊗	◓	⊗	●
◓	⊗	⊗	⊗	◓	⊗	⊗	◓	●	◓	●	⊗	◓	◓	⊗	◓	⊗	◓	◓	◓
●	●	◓	◓	◓	◓	⊗	⊗	⊗	⊗	⊗	⊗	⊗	●	●	●	⊗	●	⊗	◓
◓	◓	●	⊗	⊗	⊗	⊗	⊗	⊗	⊗	●	◓	◓	⊗	⊗	⊗	⊗	●	●	●
●	⊗	●	●	●	◓	◓	●	●	◓	◓	⊗	◓	●	⊗	◓	⊗	◓	⊗	◓
●	●	●	⊗	●	⊗	⊗	●	●	●	⊗	⊗	●	●	●	●	●	●	●	●
●	●	●	●	◓	⊗	⊗	⊗	◓	⊗	◓	◓	◓	⊗	⊗	⊗	⊗	⊗	⊗	◓
●	◓	●	●	●	◓	⊗	⊗	●	●	●	●	●	●	●	●	⊗	◓	●	●
●	◓	◓	◓	◓	◓	◓	◓	●	◓	●	●	◓	◓	◓	◓	●	●	●	●
⊗	◓	⊗	⊗	◓	◓	⊗	⊗	◓	◓	◓	●	●	◓	◓	◓	◓	◓	◓	◓
●	◓	⊗	⊗	●	◓	⊗	⊗	●	◓	●	⊗	◓	●	●	●	⊗	⊗	◓	●

KEY

- ● Major Aspect
- ◓ Minor Aspect
- ⊗ Not Applicable

Continuing Education - Non-Professional	Energy Efficient Equipment	Appropriate Technology	Passive Heating & Cooling	Solar Water Heating	Photovoltaics	Other Energy Alternatives	Energy Management	Local Indigenous Materials	Natural / Renewable Materials	Recycled / Salvaged Materials
	Efficiency Education							Materials		
Apeiron Institute	●	●	●	●	●	●	◓	●	●	●
Aprovecho Research Center	◓	●	●	●	◓	◓	◓	●	●	◓
Arcosanti	◓	●	●	◓	◓	◓	◓	⊗	◓	◓
Building Education Center	◓	⊗	⊗	⊗	●	⊗	◓	⊗	⊗	⊗
Cal-Earth Institute / Geltaftan Foundation	◓	●	●	◓	◓	⊗	◓	●	●	◓
Canelo Project	◓	●	●	◓	◓	◓	◓	●	●	●
Center for Maximum Potential Building Systems	◓	●	●	●	●	⊗	⊗	●	●	●
Cob Cottage Company	⊗	●	●	⊗	◓	◓	⊗	●	●	●
Cobworks	⊗	◓	●	⊗	◓	◓	⊗	●	●	●
DAWN Southwest	●	●	●	●	●	●	●	●	●	●
Earthwood Building School	◓	◓	◓	⊗	◓	◓	●	●	●	◓
EcoVersity	●	●	●	●	●	●	●	●	●	●
Eco-Village Training Center	●	●	●	●	●	●	●	⊗	●	●
Everdale Environmental Learning Centre	●	●	●	●	●	●	●	◓	●	●
Goshen Timber Frames	●	●	◓	●	⊗	⊗	●	●	●	●
Groundworks	⊗	◓	●	⊗	◓	⊗	⊗	●	●	●
Heartwood School for Homebuilding Crafts	◓	●	●	●	◓	●	●	●	●	◓
House Alive	⊗	●	●	◓	◓	◓	◓	●	●	◓
Joslyn Castle Institute	◓	◓	⊗	⊗	⊗	◓	◓	◓	◓	●
Kortright Centre	●	●	●	●	●	●	●	⊗	●	⊗
Kūpono Natural Builders	◓	◓	●	◓	⊗	⊗	◓	●	●	●
Montgomery College	●	●	●	●	●	●	●	●	●	●
Occidental Arts & Ecology Center	⊗	◓	◓	◓	◓	⊗	◓	◓	◓	●
O.U.R. Ecovillage	⊗	◓	◓	◓	◓	◓	◓	◓	●	●
Pangea Partnership	●	●	●	◓	◓	◓	◓	●	●	●
Rocky Mountain Workshops	◓	◓	◓	◓	◓	◓	◓	◓	◓	◓
Seven Generations Natural Builders	⊗	⊗	●	⊗	⊗	⊗	◓	●	●	●

Materials Education						IEQ						Other		Settings/Facilities					
Low / Non-Toxic Materials	Low-Embodied-Energy Materials	Wood-Use Reduction	Non-Ozone-Depleting Materials	Materials Life Cycle Analysis	Green Product Specification	Daylighting Design	Electrical Lighting Design	Healthy Building (IAQ)	Occupant Control & Comfort Systems	Natural Ventilation	Mechanical Ventilation	Environmental Arts & Crafts	Green Operations / Facility Management	Co-operative Living	Design Studios	Lodging On Site	Camping On Site	Rural	Urban / Suburban
●	●	●	●	◓	◓	●	◓	◓	◓	◓	◓	⊗	⊗	⊗	⊗	⊗	●	●	⊗
◓	◓	●	⊗	⊗	⊗	⊗	⊗	●	⊗	⊗	⊗	⊗	◓	●	⊗	●	●	●	⊗
◓	◓	◓	◓	◓	◓	●	◓	◓	◓	●	◓	●	◓	◓	◓	●	●	◓	●
⊗	◓	◓	◓	◓	◓	⊗	⊗	⊗	⊗	◓	◓	⊗	◓	⊗	⊗	⊗	◓	⊗	●
●	●	●	●	⊗	⊗	●	⊗	●	◓	●	◓	⊗	⊗	◓	◓	◓	●	●	●
●	◓	●	◓	◓	◓	●	⊗	◓	◓	●	⊗	●	⊗	●	◓	●	◓	●	⊗
●	●	●	◓	●	●	●	⊗	●	◓	●	◓	●	◓	◓	●	●	⊗	●	⊗
●	●	●	●	●	⊗	⊗	⊗	●	⊗	◓	⊗	●	⊗	◓	◓	●	●	●	⊗
●	●	●	●	◓	⊗	◓	◓	◓	⊗	●	◓	◓	⊗	●	⊗	●	●	●	⊗
●	●	●	●	●	●	●	◓	●	◓	●	◓	●	⊗	⊗	⊗	⊗	◓	●	⊗
◓	◓	◓	◓	⊗	◓	◓	⊗	◓	◓	◓	⊗	◓	⊗	⊗	⊗	●	◓	●	⊗
●	●	⊗	●	●	⊗	●	⊗	●	⊗	●	⊗	●	⊗	⊗	⊗	⊗	●	●	●
●	⊗	⊗	⊗	⊗	⊗	⊗	⊗	⊗	⊗	⊗	⊗	●	●	●	⊗	●	●	●	⊗
●	●	●	●	◓	●	●	◓	⊗	●	◓	◓	●	◓	●	⊗	●	●	●	⊗
●	●	●	●	◓	◓	●	◓	◓	◓	●	●	⊗	⊗	●	⊗	⊗	⊗	●	⊗
●	●	●	●	⊗	⊗	●	◓	●	●	●	⊗	●	⊗	●	⊗	⊗	●	●	⊗
◓	●	◓	◓	◓	◓	◓	◓	◓	◓	◓	◓	◓	⊗	◓	◓	⊗	⊗	●	⊗
●	◓	●	⊗	⊗	⊗	◓	⊗	●	⊗	◓	⊗	◓	⊗	◓	⊗	⊗	●	◓	⊗
◓	◓	◓	◓	◓	●	⊗	⊗	⊗	⊗	⊗	⊗	⊗	⊗	⊗	⊗	⊗	⊗	⊗	●
⊗	⊗	⊗	⊗	⊗	⊗	⊗	⊗	◓	⊗	◓	⊗	●	⊗	⊗	⊗	⊗	⊗	⊗	●
●	●	●	●	⊗	⊗	●	⊗	●	◓	◓	◓	◓	⊗	⊗	⊗	●	●	●	●
●	●	●	●	●	●	●	●	●	●	●	●	◓	●	◓	●	●	◓	◓	●
●	◓	◓	◓	⊗	◓	⊗	⊗	●	⊗	◓	⊗	◓	◓	●	⊗	●	●	●	⊗
●	●	●	●	◓	◓	◓	◓	◓	⊗	◓	⊗	◓	◓	●	⊗	●	●	●	◓
●	●	●	●	●	◓	◓	◓	●	◓	◓	◓	⊗	●	◓	◓	◓	◓	◓	◓
◓	◓	⊗	◓	◓	◓	◓	◓	◓	◓	◓	◓	⊗	⊗	◓	◓	●	⊗	●	⊗
●	●	●	●	◓	⊗	●	⊗	⊗	⊗	◓	⊗	⊗	⊗	⊗	⊗	●	●	●	●

KEY

- ● Major Aspect
- ◓ Minor Aspect
- ⊗ Not Applicable

Continuing Education - Non-Professional	Course Format									
	Traveling Workshops	International Courses	Owner / Builder	Hands-on Building	Design / Build	Correspondence Courses	Online Courses	College Credit	Continuing Education Credit	Internship / Apprenticeship
Apeiron Institute	●	⊗	●	●	●	⊗	⊗	◓	◓	●
Aprovecho Research Center	⊗	⊗	⊗	⊗	⊗	⊗	⊗	◓	⊗	●
Arcosanti	⊗	⊗	⊗	●	◓	●	⊗	◓	◓	●
Building Education Center	⊗	⊗	⊗	●	●	⊗	⊗	⊗	⊗	⊗
Cal-Earth Institute / Geltaftan Foundation	⊗	⊗	●	●	●	⊗	◓	⊗	⊗	●
Canelo Project	◓	●	●	●	●	⊗	⊗	⊗	⊗	●
Center for Maximum Potential Building Systems	⊗	⊗	⊗	●	●	⊗	⊗	◓	◓	●
Cob Cottage Company	●	●	●	●	●	⊗	⊗	◓	⊗	●
Cobworks	●	●	●	●	●	⊗	⊗	⊗	⊗	●
DAWN Southwest	◓	◓	●	●	●	●	⊗	⊗	⊗	●
Earthwood Building School	●	●	●	●	⊗	⊗	⊗	⊗	⊗	⊗
EcoVersity	⊗	⊗	⊗	●	●	⊗	●	⊗	●	●
Eco-Village Training Center	⊗	⊗	⊗	●	●	⊗	⊗	●	◓	●
Everdale Environmental Learning Centre	⊗	⊗	⊗	●	●	⊗	⊗	⊗	⊗	●
Goshen Timber Frames	⊗	⊗	●	●	●	⊗	⊗	⊗	●	●
Groundworks	●	●	●	●	●	⊗	⊗	⊗	⊗	⊗
Heartwood School for Homebuilding Crafts	●	◓	●	●	●	⊗	⊗	⊗	⊗	◓
House Alive	◓	◓	●	●	◓	⊗	⊗	⊗	⊗	◓
Joslyn Castle Institute	◓	●	⊗	⊗	⊗	⊗	⊗	⊗	◓	●
Kortright Centre	⊗	⊗	●	●	●	⊗	⊗	◓	⊗	◓
Kūpono Natural Builders	●	⊗	●	●	●	⊗	⊗	⊗	⊗	⊗
Montgomery College	⊗	⊗	◓	⊗	⊗	⊗	⊗	●	◓	⊗
Occidental Arts & Ecology Center	⊗	⊗	⊗	◓	⊗	⊗	⊗	⊗	⊗	●
O.U.R. Ecovillage	◓	◓	●	●	●	⊗	⊗	⊗	⊗	●
Pangea Partnership	●	●	◓	●	●	⊗	⊗	◓	◓	◓
Rocky Mountain Workshops	◓	◓	◓	●	◓	⊗	⊗	◓	◓	◓
Seven Generations Natural Builders	●	◓	●	●	●	⊗	⊗	⊗	⊗	⊗

IDP Qualification	Professional Courses	Professional Certification	Daylong / Weekend Workshop	Weeklong / Month Courses	Semester Courses	Yearlong Courses	Programs Offered Year-Round	Scholarships	Sliding-Scale Available	Work-Trade Available	Paid Internship Available	Multiple Instructors	Not-for-Profit Organization	Membership Organization	Industry / Trade Association	Accredited Academic Institution	Design Services	Consulting Services	Construction Services
Course Format (con't)								Financial					Organization						
⊗	⊗	⊗	●	⊗	⊗	⊗	●	●	●	●	●	●	●	⊗	⊗	⊗	●	●	⊗
⊗	⊗	⊗	◓	⊗	●	⊗	⊗	⊗	⊗	◓	⊗	⊗	●	●	⊗	⊗	⊗	⊗	⊗
⊗	⊗	⊗	◓	●	●	◓	●	◓	◓	●	⊗	●	⊗	⊗	⊗	⊗	⊗	⊗	⊗
⊗	⊗	⊗	●	⊗	⊗	⊗	●	⊗	⊗	⊗	⊗	⊗	●	⊗	⊗	⊗	⊗	⊗	⊗
⊗	⊗	⊗	●	●	●	⊗	●	◓	◓	⊗	⊗	◓	●	⊗	⊗	⊗	◓	◓	◓
⊗	⊗	⊗	●	●	⊗	⊗	◓	◓	◓	◓	◓	●	●	⊗	⊗	⊗	●	●	◓
⊗	◓	⊗	◓	◓	●	⊗	◓	⊗	⊗	●	●	●	●	⊗	⊗	⊗	●	●	●
⊗	●	●	◓	●	◓	◓	◓	◓	⊗	◓	◓	●	⊗	⊗	⊗	⊗	●	●	◓
⊗	⊗	⊗	●	●	●	⊗	◓	⊗	◓	◓	◓	◓	◓	⊗	◓	⊗	●	●	●
⊗	⊗	⊗	●	⊗	⊗	⊗	●	◓	◓	●	⊗	●	◓	⊗	⊗	⊗	⊗	●	⊗
⊗	⊗	⊗	●	●	⊗	⊗	◓	⊗	◓	⊗	◓	●	⊗	⊗	◓	⊗	◓	●	⊗
⊗	●	●	●	●	●	⊗	●	⊗	⊗	●	⊗	●	●	⊗	⊗	⊗	⊗	⊗	⊗
⊗	⊗	●	●	●	⊗	⊗	⊗	●	⊗	●	⊗	●	●	⊗	⊗	⊗	⊗	⊗	⊗
⊗	⊗	⊗	●	⊗	⊗	⊗	◓	⊗	●	●	●	●	●	●	⊗	⊗	⊗	⊗	⊗
⊗	⊗	⊗	⊗	●	●	⊗	●	⊗	⊗	⊗	⊗	●	⊗	⊗	●	⊗	●	●	●
⊗	⊗	⊗	●	●	⊗	⊗	◓	⊗	●	⊗	⊗	●	⊗	⊗	⊗	⊗	⊗	●	⊗
⊗	◓	⊗	◓	●	⊗	⊗	◓	⊗	⊗	⊗	◓	●	⊗	⊗	⊗	⊗	◓	◓	◓
⊗	⊗	⊗	◓	◓	⊗	⊗	◓	⊗	⊗	◓	◓	●	●	⊗	⊗	⊗	◓	●	◓
⊗	⊗	⊗	◓	⊗	⊗	⊗	◓	⊗	⊗	⊗	◓	⊗	●	◓	◓	⊗	⊗	◓	⊗
⊗	⊗	⊗	●	⊗	⊗	⊗	●	⊗	⊗	⊗	⊗	●	●	●	⊗	⊗	⊗	⊗	⊗
⊗	⊗	⊗	●	●	⊗	⊗	●	◓	◓	◓	⊗	●	⊗	⊗	⊗	⊗	●	●	●
⊗	●	⊗	⊗	⊗	●	⊗	⊗	●	⊗	⊗	⊗	●	⊗	⊗	⊗	●	◓	◓	⊗
⊗	⊗	⊗	●	◓	⊗	⊗	⊗	⊗	◓	◓	⊗	●	●	●	⊗	⊗	⊗	●	⊗
⊗	⊗	⊗	●	●	●	◓	●	◓	●	◓	⊗	●	●	◓	⊗	⊗	●	◓	◓
⊗	⊗	⊗	◓	●	⊗	⊗	◓	◓	◓	◓	◓	◓	●	⊗	⊗	⊗	●	●	●
⊗	●	◓	●	●	⊗	⊗	●	⊗	⊗	⊗	⊗	●	⊗	⊗	●	⊗	⊗	◓	●
⊗	●	⊗	●	●	⊗	⊗	●	◓	●	●	⊗	●	⊗	●	⊗	⊗	◓	●	●

KEY

● Major Aspect

◓ Minor Aspect

⊗ Not Applicable

Continuing Education - Non-Professional	Available Resources									
	Testing / Technical Services	Event Hosting	Library / Resource Room	Public Lecture Series	Newsletter / Journal	Research Publication / Books	Resource Guides	Product Sales / Promotion	Affiliation w/ College or Research	Children's Programs
Apeiron Institute	⊗	●	●	●	⊗	⊗	⊗	⊗	⊗	●
Aprovecho Research Center	⊗	⊗	⊗	⊗	●	●	◓	⊗	●	⊗
Arcosanti	⊗	●	●	⊗	◓	⊗	⊗	⊗	◓	⊗
Building Education Center	⊗	⊗	⊗	⊗	⊗	⊗	⊗	⊗	⊗	⊗
Cal-Earth Institute / Geltaftan Foundation	⊗	◓	⊗	⊗	⊗	●	⊗	●	●	●
Canelo Project	⊗	●	●	●	◓	●	●	●	⊗	◓
Center for Maximum Potential Building Systems	●	●	●	◓	⊗	●	●	⊗	●	⊗
Cob Cottage Company	⊗	◓	◓	●	●	●	◓	⊗	⊗	●
Cobworks	●	◓	◓	●	◓	⊗	◓	◓	⊗	◓
DAWN Southwest	⊗	●	●	◓	◓	⊗	◓	●	◓	⊗
Earthwood Building School	⊗	◓	●	⊗	●	●	⊗	⊗	⊗	⊗
EcoVersity	⊗	●	●	●	◓	⊗	⊗	⊗	⊗	⊗
Eco-Village Training Center	⊗	●	●	⊗	⊗	⊗	●	⊗	⊗	●
Everdale Environmental Learning Centre	⊗	●	⊗	⊗	●	⊗	⊗	●	⊗	●
Goshen Timber Frames	⊗	⊗	⊗	⊗	⊗	⊗	⊗	●	⊗	⊗
Groundworks	●	●	●	⊗	⊗	●	⊗	●	⊗	◓
Heartwood School for Homebuilding Crafts	⊗	◓	●	◓	◓	◓	◓	⊗	⊗	⊗
House Alive	⊗	⊗	⊗	⊗	⊗	⊗	⊗	⊗	⊗	⊗
Joslyn Castle Institute	⊗	●	◓	●	◓	●	◓	⊗	●	●
Kortright Centre	⊗	●	●	●	●	◓	●	●	●	●
Kūpono Natural Builders	⊗	⊗	⊗	◓	⊗	⊗	●	⊗	⊗	⊗
Montgomery College	⊗	⊗	⊗	⊗	⊗	⊗	⊗	⊗	⊗	⊗
Occidental Arts & Ecology Center	⊗	⊗	⊗	⊗	⊗	⊗	⊗	⊗	●	⊗
O.U.R. Ecovillage	⊗	●	●	●	◓	◓	◓	⊗	●	●
Pangea Partnership	◓	◓	●	●	●	◓	◓	◓	●	◓
Rocky Mountain Workshops	⊗	◓	⊗	⊗	⊗	⊗	⊗	⊗	●	⊗
Seven Generations Natural Builders	⊗	⊗	⊗	◓	⊗	⊗	⊗	⊗	⊗	⊗

Teen Programs	Demonstration Projects	Co-operation w/ other Groups	Involvement in Local Projects	Site Tours Available	Conference Sponsorship	Spiritual Framework	
Community Involvement							**Other**
●	●	●	●	●	●	●	
⊗	●	●	◓	●	⊗	⊗	
⊗	⊗	◓	⊗	●	⊗	⊗	
⊗	⊗	⊗	⊗	⊗	⊗	⊗	
●	●	◓	◓	●	◓	◓	Lunar Construction; Archemy; Ceramic Housing
◓	●	◓	●	●	◓	◓	
⊗	●	●	●	●	●	⊗	Resource Balance
◓	●	●	◓	●	◓	⊗	
◓	●	◓	●	●	⊗	◓	Educating Instructors
⊗	◓	◓	⊗	◓	⊗	⊗	
⊗	⊗	◓	◓	●	⊗	◓	
⊗	●	●	●	●	●	⊗	
⊗	●	●	●	●	●	●	Organic Gardening; Herbal Medicine
●	●	●	◓	●	⊗	⊗	
⊗	◓	◓	●	●	⊗	⊗	
◓	●	⊗	⊗	⊗	●	⊗	
⊗	◓	●	●	◓	⊗	◓	
⊗	⊗	◓	◓	●	⊗	⊗	
●	⊗	●	●	◓	◓	⊗	
●	●	◓	⊗	●	⊗	⊗	Wind; Geothermal; Environmental Programs
⊗	⊗	◓	◓	◓	⊗	●	
⊗	⊗	⊗	⊗	⊗	⊗	⊗	
⊗	●	◓	⊗	●	⊗	⊗	
●	●	●	●	●	●	●	
◓	◓	●	●	●	◓	◓	
⊗	◓	◓	◓	⊗	⊗	⊗	
⊗	◓	●	●	⊗	⊗	⊗	

KEY

- ● Major Aspect
- ◓ Minor Aspect
- ⊗ Not Applicable

	Whole Building Green Design	Green Building Rating	Residential Design / Construction	Commercial Design / Construction	Building Reuse / Renovation	Affordable Building / Housing	Participatory Design Process	Transit-Oriented Design	Reduced Development Footprint	Sustainable Community Design
Continuing Education - Non-Professional	**General Green Building**									
Shaw EcoVillage	◓	⊗	●	⊗	◓	◓	●	◓	◓	●
Solar Energy International	●	⊗	●	⊗	◓	◓	◓	⊗	◓	⊗
Solar Living Institute	●	◓	●	◓	◓	●	●	●	●	●
Southwest Solar Adobe School	◓	⊗	⊗	⊗	⊗	●	⊗	⊗	⊗	⊗
Wright Way Organic Resource Center	◓	◓	◓	◓	◓	◓	◓	◓	◓	◓
Yestermorrow Design/Build School	●	◓	●	◓	●	◓	●	⊗	⊗	●
Continuing Education - Professional										
Alaska Craftsman Home Program, Inc.	◓	◓	●	⊗	●	●	◓	⊗	⊗	◓
Boston Architectural Center	●	●	◓	◓	●	◓	◓	◓	●	◓
Chicago Center for Green Technology	●	●	●	●	●	◓	●	●	●	●
Cleveland Green Building Coalition	●	●	●	●	●	◓	●	●	◓	●
Ecosa Institute	●	◓	●	●	◓	◓	●	◓	●	●
Energy and Environmental Building Association	⊗	⊗	◓	◓	⊗	◓	⊗	⊗	⊗	⊗
Florida Solar Energy Center	●	●	●	●	◓	●	◓	◓	●	●
Green Advantage	●	◓	●	●	◓	◓	◓	◓	◓	◓
International Institute for Bau-biologie & Ecology	●	⊗	◓	◓	◓	◓	◓	◓	⊗	◓
Island School of Building Arts	◓	◓	●	●	●	●	●	⊗	◓	●
Lighting Design Lab	⊗	⊗	⊗	●	●	⊗	◓	⊗	⊗	⊗
Pacific Energy Center	●	◓	◓	●	◓	⊗	●	⊗	◓	◓
Seattle Central Community College	●	●	●	●	⊗	⊗	●	◓	◓	●
Sir Sandford Fleming College	●	●	●	●	◓	●	●	◓	●	●
Sonoma State University	●	●	◓	◓	◓	◓	◓	●	●	◓
Southface Energy Institute	●	●	●	●	●	●	●	◓	◓	●
Stockton Energy Training Center	◓	⊗	●	⊗	◓	●	⊗	⊗	⊗	⊗
Timber Framers Guild	●	⊗	●	●	◓	◓	◓	⊗	⊗	◓
US Green Building Council	●	●	◓	●	●	⊗	●	◓	◓	●

Sustainable Site Design	Stormwater Managment	Sustainable Landscaping	Permaculture	Green / Vegetated Roofing	Exterior Lighting	Dome Building	Earth Sheltering	Earthen Construction	Masonry Construction	Straw-based Construction	Timber Framing	Non-Timber-Framed Wood Construction	Site Protection / Reduced Disturbance	Deconstruction Waste Management	Construction Waste Recycling	IAQ Management	Water Efficiency	Innovative Wastewater Treatment	Energy Efficient Building Envelope
Sustainable Sites						Construction Method							Management						
●	●	●	●	●	◓	⊗	●	◓	⊗	⊗	◓	●	⊗	⊗	⊗	⊗	●	⊗	◓
◓	⊗	⊗	⊗	⊗	◓	⊗	⊗	●	◓	●	⊗	⊗	⊗	◓	◓	⊗	⊗	⊗	●
●	●	●	●	●	●	◓	●	●	◓	●	◓	●	●	●	◓	⊗	●	●	●
⊗	⊗	⊗	⊗	⊗	◓	●	⊗	●	⊗	⊗	⊗	⊗	◓	◓	◓	⊗	⊗	◓	●
●	◓	●	●	◓	◓	◓	◓	●	◓	◓	◓	◓	◓	◓	◓	◓	◓	●	◓
◓	⊗	●	⊗	◓	◓	⊗	◓	●	◓	●	●	●	⊗	●	◓	⊗	◓	●	●
◓	⊗	◓	⊗	◓	⊗	◓	◓	⊗	◓	◓	◓	●	⊗	⊗	⊗	●	◓	⊗	●
●	●	●	◓	●	●	◓	◓	◓	◓	◓	◓	◓	◓	◓	●	●	●	◓	◓
●	●	●	●	●	●	◓	◓	◓	◓	◓	◓	◓	●	●	●	●	●	●	●
●	●	◓	◓	●	◓	⊗	⊗	⊗	⊗	●	●	◓	◓	●	●	●	●	●	●
●	◓	●	●	◓	◓	◓	◓	◓	◓	◓	◓	◓	●	◓	◓	◓	●	●	●
◓	◓	⊗	⊗	⊗	⊗	⊗	⊗	⊗	⊗	⊗	●	◓	⊗	⊗	◓	●	⊗	◓	●
●	◓	●	⊗	◓	◓	⊗	⊗	⊗	●	⊗	⊗	●	◓	◓	◓	◓	●	●	●
●	◓	◓	◓	◓	◓	◓	◓	◓	◓	◓	◓	◓	●	◓	◓	◓	●	◓	●
◓	⊗	◓	⊗	◓	◓	⊗	◓	◓	◓	◓	◓	◓	⊗	⊗	◓	◓	◓	●	◓
●	⊗	⊗	⊗	◓	●	⊗	⊗	◓	⊗	⊗	●	●	◓	◓	●	⊗	⊗	⊗	◓
⊗	⊗	⊗	⊗	⊗	●	⊗	⊗	⊗	⊗	⊗	⊗	⊗	⊗	⊗	⊗	⊗	⊗	⊗	⊗
●	⊗	●	◓	●	◓	⊗	⊗	◓	⊗	●	⊗	⊗	⊗	◓	◓	◓	⊗	◓	●
●	●	⊗	⊗	●	◓	⊗	⊗	⊗	⊗	⊗	⊗	⊗	●	◓	●	●	●	●	●
●	●	●	◓	◓	◓	◓	◓	●	●	●	●	●	●	◓	●	●	●	●	●
◓	●	◓	◓	◓	●	⊗	⊗	◓	◓	◓	⊗	◓	●	●	●	●	◓	●	●
●	◓	◓	◓	◓	◓	⊗	◓	⊗	●	⊗	◓	●	◓	◓	◓	◓	●	◓	●
◓	⊗	⊗	⊗	⊗	⊗	⊗	⊗	⊗	⊗	⊗	⊗	⊗	⊗	◓	◓	◓	◓	⊗	●
◓	⊗	◓	⊗	⊗	◓	⊗	⊗	⊗	⊗	◓	●	●	◓	●	◓	⊗	⊗	⊗	●
●	◓	◓	◓	◓	◓	⊗	◓	⊗	◓	⊗	◓	◓	◓	◓	◓	●	●	◓	◓

KEY

- ● Major Aspect
- ◓ Minor Aspect
- ⊗ Not Applicable

	Efficiency Education							Materials		
	Energy Efficient Equipment	Appropriate Technology	Passive Heating & Cooling	Solar Water Heating	Photovoltaics	Other Energy Alternatives	Energy Management	Local Indigenous Materials	Natural / Renewable Materials	Recycled / Salvaged Materials
Continuing Education - Non-Professional										
Shaw EcoVillage	◓	◓	●	⊗	⊗	◓	◓	◓	◓	●
Solar Energy International	●	◓	●	●	●	●	●	●	●	◓
Solar Living Institute	●	●	●	●	●	●	●	●	●	●
Southwest Solar Adobe School	◓	●	●	⊗	⊗	⊗	⊗	●	●	●
Wright Way Organic Resource Center	●	●	◓	◓	◓	◓	◓	◓	◓	◓
Yestermorrow Design/Build School	⊗	◓	●	●	◓	◓	⊗	●	●	●
Continuing Education - Professional										
Alaska Craftsman Home Program, Inc.	●	●	◓	◓	⊗	◓	◓	⊗	⊗	⊗
Boston Architectural Center	◓	●	◓	◓	◓	●	◓	●	●	●
Chicago Center for Green Technology	●	●	●	●	●	●	●	●	●	●
Cleveland Green Building Coalition	●	●	●	●	●	●	●	◓	◓	●
Ecosa Institute	●	●	●	●	●	◓	●	●	●	●
Energy and Environmental Building Association	●	●	◓	◓	◓	◓	◓	⊗	⊗	◓
Green Advantage	●	●	●	◓	◓	◓	◓	◓	◓	●
Florida Solar Energy Center	●	●	●	●	●	●	●	◓	◓	◓
International Institute for Bau-biologie & Ecology	◓	◓	●	●	●	◓	◓	◓	●	◓
Island School of Building Arts	◓	⊗	⊗	⊗	⊗	⊗	◓	●	●	●
Lighting Design Lab	◓	⊗	⊗	⊗	⊗	◓	◓	⊗	⊗	⊗
Pacific Energy Center	●	●	●	◓	●	●	●	⊗	●	●
Seattle Central Community College	●	⊗	●	●	●	⊗	◓	●	●	●
Sir Sandford Fleming College	●	●	●	●	●	●	●	●	●	●
Sonoma State University	◓	◓	◓	◓	◓	⊗	●	◓	●	◓
Southface Energy Institute	◓	●	●	●	●	●	●	◓	◓	●
Stockton Energy Training Center	●	◓	◓	◓	◓	⊗	●	⊗	⊗	◓
Timber Framers Guild	⊗	◓	◓	⊗	⊗	⊗	⊗	●	●	●
US Green Building Council	◓	◓	◓	◓	◓	◓	◓	◓	◓	◓

Low / Non-Toxic Materials	Low-Embodied-Energy Materials	Wood-Use Reduction	Non-Ozone-Depleting Materials	Materials Life Cycle Analysis	Green Product Specification	Daylighting Design	Electrical Lighting Design	Healthy Building (IAQ)	Occupant Control & Comfort Systems	Natural Ventilation	Mechanical Ventilation	Environmental Arts & Crafts	Green Operations / Facility Management	Co-operative Living	Design Studios	Lodging On Site	Camping On Site	Rural	Urban / Suburban
Materials Education						IEQ						Other		Settings/Facilities					
●	⊗	◓	◓	⊗	⊗	⊗	⊗	⊗	⊗	⊗	⊗	●	⊗	⊗	⊗	⊗	⊗	⊗	●
◓	●	◓	◓	⊗	●	◓	⊗	◓	●	◓	⊗	⊗	⊗	⊗	⊗	⊗	⊗	●	◓
●	●	●	◓	⊗	●	●	●	●	◓	●	◓	◓	●	●	⊗	⊗	◓	◓	⊗
●	●	●	●	◓	◓	⊗	◓	⊗	◓	◓	⊗	●	⊗	⊗	●	⊗	◓	⊗	⊗
◓	◓	◓	◓	◓	◓	◓	◓	◓	◓	◓	◓	●	◓	◓	●	◓	◓	●	⊗
◓	●	⊗	⊗	◓	⊗	◓	⊗	●	⊗	⊗	⊗	●	⊗	●	●	●	●	●	⊗
◓	◓	◓	⊗	◓	⊗	◓	◓	●	●	◓	●	⊗	⊗	⊗	⊗	⊗	⊗	⊗	◓
●	●	●	●	●	●	◓	●	●	●	◓	◓	⊗	◓	⊗	●	⊗	⊗	⊗	●
●	●	●	●	●	●	●	◓	●	●	●	●	●	●	⊗	⊗	⊗	⊗	⊗	●
◓	◓	◓	◓	◓	●	●	●	●	●	●	●	⊗	◓	◓	⊗	⊗	⊗	⊗	◓
●	●	◓	◓	◓	●	●	◓	●	◓	●	◓	⊗	⊗	●	●	◓	⊗	◓	◓
◓	⊗	⊗	⊗	⊗	◓	◓	⊗	●	◓	⊗	●	⊗	⊗	⊗	⊗	⊗	⊗	⊗	⊗
◓	◓	◓	⊗	◓	◓	●	●	●	●	●	●	⊗	⊗	⊗	⊗	⊗	⊗	⊗	●
◓	◓	◓	◓	◓	●	●	◓	◓	◓	◓	◓	⊗	◓	⊗	⊗	⊗	⊗	⊗	⊗
●	◓	⊗	◓	◓	⊗	●	◓	●	◓	●	◓	⊗	⊗	⊗	⊗	⊗	⊗	⊗	◓
◓	◓	◓	⊗	⊗	◓	⊗	⊗	⊗	⊗	⊗	⊗	◓	⊗	⊗	⊗	⊗	⊗	●	⊗
⊗	⊗	⊗	⊗	⊗	◓	●	●	⊗	⊗	⊗	⊗	⊗	◓	⊗	⊗	⊗	⊗	⊗	●
●	●	◓	⊗	●	●	●	●	●	●	●	●	⊗	●	⊗	⊗	⊗	⊗	⊗	●
●	●	●	●	●	●	●	●	●	●	●	●	⊗	●	⊗	⊗	⊗	⊗	⊗	⊗
●	●	●	●	●	●	●	●	●	●	●	●	●	◓	⊗	⊗	⊗	⊗	●	⊗
◓	●	●	●	●	●	●	◓	◓	●	●	◓	⊗	⊗	⊗	●	⊗	⊗	⊗	●
●	◓	◓	◓	◓	◓	⊗	⊗	●	⊗	⊗	⊗	⊗	⊗	◓	⊗	⊗	⊗	⊗	●
⊗	⊗	◓	⊗	⊗	⊗	◓	◓	●	◓	●	●	⊗	⊗	⊗	⊗	⊗	⊗	⊗	●
◓	◓	●	◓	●	●	⊗	⊗	⊗	⊗	◓	◓	◓	⊗	⊗	◓	⊗	◓	◓	⊗
◓	◓	◓	◓	●	◓	◓	◓	●	◓	◓	◓	⊗	●	⊗	⊗	⊗	⊗	⊗	⊗

KEY
- ● Major Aspect
- ◒ Minor Aspect
- ⊗ Not Applicable

	Course Format									
	Traveling Workshops	International Courses	Owner / Builder	Hands-on Building	Design / Build	Correspondence Courses	Online Courses	College Credit	Continuing Education Credit	Internship / Apprenticeship
Continuing Education - Non-Professional										
Shaw EcoVillage	⊗	⊗	⊗	●	●	⊗	⊗	◒	⊗	●
Solar Energy International	◒	◒	●	●	●	●	●	⊗	⊗	●
Solar Living Institute	◒	⊗	●	●	●	◒	⊗	◒	◒	●
Southwest Solar Adobe School	●	⊗	●	●	●	⊗	⊗	⊗	⊗	⊗
Wright Way Organic Resource Center	◒	◒	⊗	●	⊗	⊗	⊗	◒	◒	●
Yestermorrow Design/Build School	⊗	◒	●	●	●	⊗	⊗	◒	◒	●
Continuing Education - Professional										
Alaska Craftsman Home Program, Inc.	●	⊗	⊗	⊗	⊗	⊗	⊗	⊗	●	⊗
Boston Architectural Center	◒	◒	⊗	⊗	⊗	⊗	●	●	●	⊗
Chicago Center for Green Technology	⊗	⊗	●	⊗	●	⊗	⊗	⊗	●	●
Cleveland Green Building Coalition	⊗	⊗	●	●	⊗	⊗	⊗	⊗	●	●
Ecosa Institute	◒	⊗	⊗	◒	⊗	⊗	⊗	◒	⊗	⊗
Energy and Environmental Building Association	⊗	⊗	⊗	⊗	●	⊗	●	⊗	●	⊗
Florida Solar Energy Center	●	⊗	⊗	⊗	⊗	⊗	⊗	⊗	●	⊗
Green Advantage	⊗	⊗	⊗	⊗	⊗	⊗	⊗	●	●	⊗
International Institute for Bau-biologie & Ecology	●	⊗	⊗	⊗	⊗	●	●	⊗	◒	⊗
Island School of Building Arts	●	●	●	●	●	⊗	⊗	⊗	⊗	◒
Lighting Design Lab	●	⊗	⊗	⊗	⊗	⊗	⊗	⊗	●	⊗
Pacific Energy Center	⊗	⊗	●	⊗	●	⊗	◒	⊗	●	⊗
Seattle Central Community College	⊗	⊗	⊗	⊗	⊗	⊗	⊗	⊗	●	⊗
Sir Sandford Fleming College	⊗	⊗	⊗	●	●	⊗	⊗	●	⊗	⊗
Sonoma State University	⊗	⊗	⊗	⊗	⊗	⊗	⊗	●	●	⊗
Southface Energy Institute	●	⊗	●	●	◒	⊗	⊗	⊗	●	●
Stockton Energy Training Center	◒	●	⊗	⊗	⊗	⊗	⊗	⊗	◒	⊗
Timber Framers Guild	●	●	◒	●	●	◒	◒	⊗	●	●
US Green Building Council	●	⊗	◒	⊗	◒	⊗	◒	⊗	●	◒

IDP Qualification	Professional Courses	Professional Certification	Daylong / Weekend Workshop	Weeklong / Month Courses	Semester Courses	Yearlong Courses	Programs Offered Year-Round	Scholarships	Sliding-Scale Available	Work-Trade Available	Paid Internship Available	Multiple Instructors	Not-for-Profit Organization	Membership Organization	Industry / Trade Association	Accredited Academic Institution	Design Services	Consulting Services	Construction Services
Course Format (con't)								Financial				Organization							
⊗	⊗	⊗	⊗	⊗	●	●	●	●	●	◓	●	⊗	●	⊗	⊗	⊗	●	◓	◓
⊗	●	●	●	●	⊗	⊗	●	◓	◓	●	⊗	●	●	●	⊗	⊗	⊗	◓	⊗
⊗	●	●	●	●	⊗	⊗	⊗	◓	◓	●	⊗	●	◓	●	⊗	⊗	◓	◓	⊗
⊗	⊗	⊗	⊗	⊗	⊗	⊗	⊗	⊗	⊗	◓	⊗	⊗	⊗	⊗	⊗	⊗	⊗	⊗	⊗
◓	◓	⊗	●	⊗	⊗	⊗	◓	●	●	●	◓	●	●	⊗	⊗	⊗	●	●	◓
◓	●	●	●	●	⊗	⊗	●	●	⊗	●	●	●	●	⊗	⊗	●	⊗	⊗	⊗
⊗	◓	⊗	●	⊗	⊗	⊗	●	⊗	⊗	⊗	⊗	●	●	◓	◓	⊗	⊗	●	⊗
●	●	●	●	◓	●	⊗	●	⊗	⊗	⊗	⊗	●	●	⊗	⊗	●	⊗	⊗	⊗
⊗	●	●	●	●	⊗	⊗	●	⊗	⊗	⊗	●	●	●	⊗	⊗	⊗	⊗	⊗	⊗
⊗	●	●	●	●	⊗	⊗	●	●	⊗	⊗	⊗	◓	●	●	⊗	⊗	⊗	●	⊗
⊗	◓	◓	⊗	◓	●	⊗	●	◓	⊗	⊗	⊗	●	●	⊗	⊗	◓	●	●	◓
⊗	◓	●	⊗	⊗	⊗	⊗	●	⊗	⊗	⊗	⊗	●	●	●	⊗	◓	⊗	⊗	⊗
⊗	⊗	⊗	●	⊗	⊗	⊗	⊗	⊗	⊗	⊗	⊗	●	⊗	⊗	⊗	●	⊗	●	⊗
⊗	●	●	●	●	●	⊗	⊗	⊗	⊗	⊗	⊗	⊗	●	⊗	⊗	⊗	⊗	●	⊗
⊗	●	●	●	●	⊗	⊗	●	⊗	⊗	⊗	⊗	●	●	●	⊗	⊗	⊗	●	⊗
●	●	⊗	⊗	◓	●	⊗	●	⊗	⊗	◓	●	◓	⊗	⊗	●	⊗	◓	◓	◓
⊗	●	⊗	●	⊗	⊗	●	◓	⊗	⊗	⊗	⊗	●	◓	⊗	⊗	⊗	⊗	●	⊗
⊗	●	⊗	●	⊗	⊗	⊗	●	⊗	⊗	⊗	⊗	●	⊗	⊗	⊗	⊗	⊗	●	⊗
⊗	◓	●	⊗	⊗	⊗	●	⊗	⊗	⊗	⊗	⊗	●	⊗	⊗	⊗	●	⊗	⊗	⊗
⊗	◓	●	◓	⊗	◓	◓	⊗	●	⊗	⊗	⊗	●	⊗	⊗	⊗	●	⊗	⊗	⊗
⊗	●	●	⊗	⊗	⊗	●	●	⊗	⊗	⊗	⊗	●	⊗	⊗	⊗	●	●	●	●
⊗	●	●	●	◓	⊗	⊗	●	●	⊗	⊗	●	●	●	●	◓	⊗	◓	●	⊗
⊗	◓	⊗	●	◓	⊗	⊗	◓	⊗	⊗	⊗	⊗	●	⊗	⊗	⊗	⊗	⊗	◓	⊗
⊗	●	⊗	●	●	⊗	⊗	●	●	◓	◓	◓	●	●	●	◓	⊗	●	◓	◓
●	●	●	●	⊗	⊗	⊗	●	◓	⊗	⊗	◓	●	●	●	⊗	⊗	⊗	⊗	⊗

KEY
- ● Major Aspect
- ◓ Minor Aspect
- ⊗ Not Applicable

Available Resources

Continuing Education - Non-Professional	Testing / Technical Services	Event Hosting	Library / Resource Room	Public Lecture Series	Newsletter / Journal	Research Publication / Books	Resource Guides	Product Sales / Promotion	Affiliation w/ College or Research	Children's Programs
Shaw EcoVillage	⊗	◓	⊗	◓	⊗	⊗	⊗	◓	●	●
Solar Energy International	●	◓	◓	⊗	●	⊗	⊗	◓	⊗	●
Solar Living Institute	⊗	●	◓	●	●	◓	◓	◓	⊗	●
Southwest Solar Adobe School	⊗	⊗	⊗	⊗	●	●	⊗	⊗	⊗	⊗
Wright Way Organic Resource Center	⊗	●	●	●	●	◓	◓	◓	◓	●
Yestermorrow Design/Build School	⊗	◓	●	●	◓	⊗	⊗	⊗	●	◓

Continuing Education - Professional	Testing / Technical Services	Event Hosting	Library / Resource Room	Public Lecture Series	Newsletter / Journal	Research Publication / Books	Resource Guides	Product Sales / Promotion	Affiliation w/ College or Research	Children's Programs
Alaska Craftsman Home Program, Inc.	●	⊗	◓	⊗	⊗	◓	◓	⊗	⊗	⊗
Boston Architectural Center	⊗	◓	●	⊗	◓	⊗	⊗	⊗	⊗	⊗
Chicago Center for Green Technology	⊗	●	●	●	⊗	⊗	●	⊗	●	●
Cleveland Green Building Coalition	⊗	●	◓	●	●	◓	◓	⊗	◓	⊗
Ecosa Institute	⊗	◓	◓	⊗	◓	⊗	⊗	⊗	◓	⊗
Energy and Environmental Building Association	⊗	⊗	●	●	⊗	●	⊗	⊗	⊗	⊗
Florida Solar Energy Center	●	●	●	⊗	●	●	●	⊗	●	●
Green Advantage	●	⊗	⊗	⊗	⊗	⊗	⊗	●	●	⊗
International Institute for Bau-biologie & Ecology	◓	⊗	⊗	◓	◓	⊗	●	◓	◓	⊗
Island School of Building Arts	⊗	◓	◓	◓	⊗	◓	⊗	◓	⊗	⊗
Lighting Design Lab	⊗	◓	◓	◓	◓	◓	◓	⊗	◓	⊗
Pacific Energy Center	●	●	●	●	⊗	●	●	⊗	⊗	⊗
Seattle Central Community College	●	⊗	⊗	⊗	⊗	⊗	⊗	⊗	●	⊗
Sir Sandford Fleming College	⊗	◓	●	◓	⊗	⊗	⊗	⊗	●	⊗
Sonoma State University	⊗	●	◓	●	⊗	⊗	◓	⊗	●	⊗
Southface Energy Institute	●	●	●	●	●	●	●	◓	●	◓
Stockton Energy Training Center	⊗	●	◓	◓	⊗	⊗	◓	⊗	⊗	⊗
Timber Framers Guild	◓	●	⊗	●	●	●	●	●	⊗	⊗
US Green Building Council	⊗	⊗	⊗	◓	●	●	●	●	◓	⊗

Teen Programs	Demonstration Projects	Co-operation w/ other Groups	Involvement in Local Projects	Site Tours Available	Conference Sponsorship	Spiritual Framework	
Community Involvement							Other
●	●	●	●	●	⊗	⊗	
●	●	●	●	●	⊗	⊗	
●	●	●	●	●	●	⊗	
⊗	⊗	●	⊗	⊗	⊗	⊗	
●	●	●	◓	◓	◓	◓	
◓	●	●	●	●	◓	⊗	Design/Build Process
⊗	●	◓	◓	◓	⊗	⊗	
◓	⊗	◓	⊗	⊗	⊗	●	
●	●	●	●	●	⊗	⊗	
⊗	●	●	●	●	●	⊗	
⊗	◓	◓	●	●	⊗	◓	
⊗	⊗	◓	⊗	⊗	⊗	⊗	AIA accredited courses
●	●	●	●	●	●	⊗	Moisture Control; Green Standards
⊗	⊗	●	⊗	⊗	⊗	⊗	
⊗	⊗	●	⊗	◓	⊗	⊗	Building Biology Rating/Standards/Guidelines; Feng Shui
◓	●	◓	◓	◓	⊗	⊗	
⊗	◓	◓	◓	◓	⊗	⊗	
⊗	●	●	●	●	●	⊗	All Classes are FREE; Measurement Tool lending
⊗	⊗	⊗	⊗	⊗	⊗	⊗	
⊗	⊗	◓	●	◓	⊗	⊗	
◓	●	●	●	●	●	⊗	
◓	●	●	●	●	●	⊗	EarthCraft House program; Smart Growth; Energy Policy
⊗	◓	◓	◓	◓	◓	⊗	Publically Funded Energy Efficiency
⊗	●	●	●	⊗	●	◓	
⊗	⊗	●	◓	⊗	●	⊗	

KEY
- ● Major Aspect
- ◓ Minor Aspect
- ⊗ Not Applicable

Available Resources

Continuing Education - Non-Professional	Testing / Technical Services	Event Hosting	Library / Resource Room	Public Lecture Series	Newsletter / Journal	Research Publication / Books	Resource Guides	Product Sales / Promotion	Affiliation w/ College or Research	Children's Programs
Shaw EcoVillage	⊗	◓	⊗	◓	⊗	⊗	⊗	◓	●	●
Solar Energy International	●	◓	◓	⊗	●	⊗	⊗	◓	⊗	●
Solar Living Institute	⊗	●	◓	●	●	◓	◓	◓	⊗	●
Southwest Solar Adobe School	⊗	⊗	⊗	⊗	●	●	⊗	⊗	⊗	⊗
Wright Way Organic Resource Center	⊗	●	●	●	●	◓	◓	◓	◓	●
Yestermorrow Design/Build School	⊗	◓	●	●	◓	⊗	⊗	⊗	●	◓

Continuing Education - Professional	Testing / Technical Services	Event Hosting	Library / Resource Room	Public Lecture Series	Newsletter / Journal	Research Publication / Books	Resource Guides	Product Sales / Promotion	Affiliation w/ College or Research	Children's Programs
Alaska Craftsman Home Program, Inc.	●	⊗	◓	⊗	⊗	◓	◓	⊗	⊗	⊗
Boston Architectural Center	⊗	◓	●	⊗	◓	⊗	⊗	⊗	⊗	⊗
Chicago Center for Green Technology	⊗	●	●	●	⊗	⊗	●	⊗	●	●
Cleveland Green Building Coalition	⊗	●	◓	●	●	◓	◓	⊗	◓	⊗
Ecosa Institute	⊗	◓	◓	⊗	◓	⊗	⊗	⊗	◓	⊗
Energy and Environmental Building Association	⊗	⊗	●	●	⊗	●	⊗	⊗	⊗	⊗
Florida Solar Energy Center	●	●	●	⊗	●	●	●	⊗	●	●
Green Advantage	●	⊗	⊗	⊗	⊗	⊗	⊗	●	●	⊗
International Institute for Bau-biologie & Ecology	◓	⊗	⊗	◓	◓	⊗	●	◓	◓	⊗
Island School of Building Arts	⊗	◓	◓	◓	⊗	◓	⊗	◓	⊗	⊗
Lighting Design Lab	⊗	◓	◓	◓	◓	◓	◓	⊗	◓	⊗
Pacific Energy Center	●	●	●	●	⊗	●	●	⊗	⊗	⊗
Seattle Central Community College	●	⊗	⊗	⊗	⊗	⊗	⊗	⊗	●	⊗
Sir Sandford Fleming College	⊗	◓	●	◓	⊗	⊗	⊗	⊗	●	⊗
Sonoma State University	⊗	●	◓	●	⊗	⊗	◓	⊗	●	⊗
Southface Energy Institute	●	●	●	●	●	●	●	◓	●	◓
Stockton Energy Training Center	⊗	●	◓	◓	⊗	⊗	◓	⊗	⊗	⊗
Timber Framers Guild	◓	●	⊗	●	●	●	●	●	⊗	⊗
US Green Building Council	⊗	⊗	⊗	◓	●	●	●	●	◓	⊗

Teen Programs	Demonstration Projects	Co-operation w/ other Groups	Involvement in Local Projects	Site Tours Available	Conference Sponsorship	Spiritual Framework	
Community Involvement							**Other**
●	●	●	●	●	⊗	⊗	
●	●	●	●	●	⊗	⊗	
●	●	●	●	●	●	⊗	
⊗	⊗	●	⊗	⊗	⊗	⊗	
●	●	●	◒	◒	◒	◒	
◒	●	●	●	●	◒	⊗	Design/Build Process
⊗	●	◒	◒	◒	⊗	⊗	
◒	⊗	◒	⊗	⊗	⊗	●	
●	●	●	●	●	⊗	⊗	
⊗	●	●	●	●	●	⊗	
⊗	◒	◒	●	●	⊗	◒	
⊗	⊗	◒	⊗	⊗	⊗	⊗	AIA accredited courses
●	●	●	●	●	●	⊗	Moisture Control; Green Standards
⊗	⊗	●	⊗	⊗	⊗	⊗	
⊗	⊗	●	⊗	◒	⊗	⊗	Building Biology Rating/Standards/Guidelines; Feng Shui
◒	●	◒	◒	◒	⊗	⊗	
⊗	◒	◒	◒	◒	⊗	⊗	
⊗	●	●	●	●	●	⊗	All Classes are FREE; Measurement Tool lending
⊗	⊗	⊗	⊗	⊗	⊗	⊗	
⊗	⊗	◒	●	◒	⊗	⊗	
◒	●	●	●	●	●	⊗	
◒	●	●	●	●	●	⊗	EarthCraft House program; Smart Growth; Energy Policy
⊗	◒	◒	◒	◒	◒	⊗	Publically Funded Energy Efficiency
⊗	●	●	●	⊗	●	◒	
⊗	⊗	●	◒	⊗	●	⊗	

KEY

- ● Major Aspect
- ◓ Minor Aspect
- ⊗ Not Applicable

Higher Education	General Green Building									
	Whole Building Green Design	Green Building Rating	Residential Design / Construction	Commercial Design / Construction	Building Reuse / Renovation	Affordable Building / Housing	Participatory Design Process	Transit-Oriented Design	Reduced Development Footprint	Sustainable Community Design
Ball State University	●	◓	◓	◓	⊗	◓	◓	◓	●	●
California State Polytechnic Institute (Pomona)	◓	⊗	◓	◓	◓	◓	●	◓	●	●
California State Polytechnic Institute (San Luis Obispo)	◓	⊗	●	●	◓	◓	◓	◓	◓	◓
Carnegie Mellon University	●	●	◓	●	◓	◓	●	◓	◓	●
Colorado State University (Fort Collins)	⊗	●	◓	●	◓	◓	●	⊗	⊗	◓
Merritt College	●	◓	◓	◓	●	◓	●	●	●	●
New College of California	●	⊗	●	◓	◓	●	●	◓	●	●
San Francisco Institute of Architecture	●	⊗	●	●	●	●	●	◓	⊗	●
University of British Columbia	◓	●	◓	◓	◓	◓	●	●	●	●
University of Calgary	●	◓	●	●	◓	◓	◓	◓	◓	●
University of Florida	●	●	●	●	●	●	●	⊗	⊗	●
University of Minnesota	●	●	●	●	●	◓	●	●	●	●
University of Oregon	●	●	◓	●	●	●	●	●	●	●
University of Southern California	●	●	◓	◓	●	●	●	◓	◓	◓
University of Texas (Austin)	●	◓	◓	●	◓	●	◓	●	●	●
University of Virginia	●	◓	◓	◓	◓	◓	◓	◓	◓	●

Sustainable Site Design	Stormwater Managment	Sustainable Landscaping	Permaculture	Green / Vegetated Roofing	Exterior Lighting	Dome Building	Earth Sheltering	Earthen Construction	Masonry Construction	Straw-based Construction	Timber Framing	Non-Timber-Framed Wood Construction	Site Protection / Reduced Disturbance	Deconstruction Waste Management	Construction Waste Recycling	IAQ Management	Water Efficiency	Innovative Wastewater Treatment	Energy Efficient Building Envelope
Sustainable Sites						Construction Method							Management						
●	●	●	◓	●	●	⊗	◓	◓	◓	◓	◓	◓	◓	◓	⊗	●	●	●	●
●	●	●	●	◓	⊗	⊗	⊗	⊗	⊗	◓	⊗	⊗	◓	◓	◓	⊗	●	●	●
◓	⊗	◓	◓	◓	⊗	⊗	⊗	⊗	◓	◓	◓	◓	⊗	⊗	⊗	⊗	◓	◓	●
●	⊗	◓	⊗	●	●	⊗	⊗	⊗	●	⊗	●	●	●	⊗	◓	●	●	◓	●
⊗	⊗	⊗	⊗	◓	⊗	⊗	⊗	◓	⊗	◓	◓	●	⊗	◓	●	●	◓	⊗	●
●	●	●	◓	◓	◓	⊗	◓	◓	⊗	◓	⊗	●	●	●	●	◓	●	●	●
●	◓	◓	◓	◓	⊗	◓	◓	●	◓	●	◓	◓	◓	◓	⊗	⊗	◓	◓	●
●	●	●	●	●	●	●	●	●	●	●	●	●	●	●	●	●	●	●	●
●	◓	◓	◓	◓	◓	⊗	◓	◓	●	◓	●	⊗	⊗	⊗	⊗	⊗	◓	◓	●
◓	◓	●	◓	◓	◓	⊗	◓	⊗	●	◓	◓	●	◓	◓	◓	●	◓	⊗	●
●	●	●	⊗	●	●	⊗	⊗	●	●	⊗	●	●	●	●	●	●	●	●	●
●	◓	●	◓	◓	◓	⊗	◓	⊗	◓	⊗	◓	◓	●	●	●	●	●	◓	●
●	●	●	●	●	●	◓	◓	◓	●	◓	●	●	●	●	●	●	●	●	●
●	●	●	◓	◓	◓	◓	●	◓	◓	◓	◓	◓	◓	●	●	◓	◓	◓	◓
●	●	●	⊗	◓	◓	◓	◓	◓	◓	◓	◓	◓	⊗	⊗	⊗	●	●	●	●
●	◓	●	⊗	◓	◓	⊗	◓	◓	◓	◓	◓	◓	◓	◓	◓	◓	◓	◓	●

KEY

● Major Aspect

◒ Minor Aspect

⊗ Not Applicable

Higher Education	Traveling Workshops	International Courses	Owner / Builder	Hands-on Building	Design / Build	Correspondence Courses	Online Courses	College Credit	Continuing Education Credit	Internship / Apprenticeship
	Course Format									
Ball State University	⊗	⊗	⊗	⊗	⊗	⊗	⊗	●	⊗	⊗
California State Polytechnic Institute (Pomona)	⊗	⊗	⊗	⊗	⊗	⊗	⊗	●	⊗	●
California State Polytechnic Institute (San Luis Obispo)	◒	●	⊗	◒	◒	⊗	⊗	●	⊗	●
Carnegie Mellon University	⊗	●	⊗	●	●	⊗	⊗	●	◒	◒
Colorado State University (Fort Collins)	◒	⊗	⊗	⊗	⊗	⊗	⊗	●	◒	⊗
Merritt College	⊗	⊗	⊗	●	●	⊗	⊗	●	⊗	●
New College of California	⊗	◒	⊗	●	●	⊗	⊗	●	⊗	◒
San Francisco Institute of Architecture	●	●	⊗	●	●	●	●	●	●	●
University of British Columbia	⊗	◒	⊗	⊗	◒	⊗	⊗	●	⊗	⊗
University of Calgary	⊗	⊗	⊗	⊗	⊗	⊗	⊗	●	⊗	⊗
University of Florida	●	⊗	⊗	⊗	⊗	⊗	●	●	●	●
University of Minnesota	⊗	⊗	⊗	◒	⊗	⊗	⊗	●	●	⊗
University of Oregon	●	●	◒	●	●	●	●	●	●	●
University of Southern California	⊗	⊗	⊗	⊗	⊗	⊗	⊗	●	●	●
University of Texas (Austin)	●	●	⊗	●	●	⊗	⊗	●	◒	◒
University of Virginia	⊗	●	⊗	⊗	●	⊗	⊗	●	⊗	⊗

IDP Qualification	Professional Courses	Professional Certification	Daylong / Weekend Workshop	Weeklong / Month Courses	Semester Courses	Yearlong Courses	Programs Offered Year-Round	Scholarships	Sliding-Scale Available	Work-Trade Available	Paid Internship Available	Multiple Instructors	Not-for-Profit Organization	Membership Organization	Industry / Trade Association	Accredited Academic Institution	Design Services	Consulting Services	Construction Services
Course Format (con't)								Financial					Organization						
⊗	●	⊗	⊗	⊗	●	⊗	●	●	⊗	⊗	⊗	●	⊗	⊗	⊗	●	●	●	⊗
⊗	⊗	⊗	●	⊗	⊗	⊗	●	⊗	⊗	⊗	⊗	●	⊗	⊗	⊗	●	⊗	⊗	⊗
⊗	◒	●	◒	◒	●	●	●	◒	⊗	⊗	⊗	●	⊗	⊗	⊗	●	◒	◒	⊗
⊗	●	●	●	⊗	●	●	⊗	●	⊗	⊗	●	⊗	⊗	⊗	⊗	●	●	●	⊗
⊗	◒	●	◒	⊗	⊗	⊗	⊗	◒	⊗	⊗	●	●	⊗	⊗	⊗	●	⊗	●	⊗
⊗	⊗	●	●	⊗	●	⊗	●	●	⊗	⊗	◒	●	⊗	⊗	⊗	●	◒	◒	◒
⊗	⊗	●	◒	⊗	⊗	●	●	●	⊗	●	⊗	●	●	⊗	⊗	●	◒	◒	⊗
⊗	●	●	●	●	●	●	●	●	⊗	●	⊗	●	●	⊗	⊗	⊗	●	●	⊗
⊗	●	●	⊗	⊗	●	⊗	●	⊗	⊗	⊗	⊗	●	⊗	⊗	⊗	●	⊗	⊗	⊗
⊗	⊗	⊗	⊗	⊗	●	⊗	⊗	●	⊗	⊗	⊗	●	⊗	⊗	⊗	●	⊗	⊗	⊗
⊗	●	●	●	●	●	●	●	⊗	⊗	⊗	⊗	●	⊗	⊗	⊗	●	⊗	●	●
⊗	●	●	●	⊗	●	⊗	●	⊗	⊗	⊗	⊗	⊗	●	⊗	⊗	●	◒	●	⊗
●	●	●	●	●	●	●	●	●	⊗	⊗	●	●	⊗	⊗	⊗	●	●	●	●
⊗	⊗	●	⊗	⊗	●	⊗	●	●	⊗	⊗	●	●	⊗	⊗	⊗	●	⊗	●	⊗
●	◒	●	●	◒	●	●	●	◒	⊗	⊗	◒	●	⊗	⊗	⊗	●	⊗	●	⊗
⊗	⊗	⊗	⊗	⊗	●	⊗	⊗	●	⊗	⊗	⊗	●	⊗	⊗	⊗	●	⊗	⊗	⊗

KEY
● Major Aspect
◒ Minor Aspect
⊗ Not Applicable

Higher Education	Testing / Technical Services	Event Hosting	Library / Resource Room	Public Lecture Series	Newsletter / Journal	Research Publication / Books	Resource Guides	Product Sales / Promotion	Affiliation w/ College or Research	Children's Programs
	Available Resources									
Ball State University	●	●	●	●	◒	●	◒	⊗	●	⊗
California State Polytechnic Institute (Pomona)	⊗	◒	◒	◒	◒	◒	⊗	⊗	●	⊗
California State Polytechnic Institute (San Luis Obispo)	◒	◒	●	●	◒	◒	◒	⊗	●	⊗
Carnegie Mellon University	●	◒	●	●	⊗	●	⊗	⊗	●	⊗
Colorado State University (Fort Collins)	⊗	⊗	◒	⊗	⊗	⊗	◒	⊗	●	⊗
Merritt College	⊗	●	◒	◒	◒	⊗	◒	⊗	●	⊗
New College of California	⊗	●	●	●	⊗	●	⊗	⊗	●	⊗
San Francisco Institute of Architecture	⊗	●	●	●	⊗	●	⊗	⊗	●	⊗
University of British Columbia	⊗	◒	●	◒	◒	⊗	⊗	⊗	●	⊗
University of Calgary	⊗	⊗	●	⊗	⊗	●	⊗	⊗	●	⊗
University of Florida	⊗	●	●	●	⊗	●	●	⊗	●	⊗
University of Minnesota	⊗	◒	◒	◒	⊗	●	●	⊗	●	⊗
University of Oregon	●	●	●	●	●	●	●	⊗	●	●
University of Southern California	⊗	⊗	●	●	⊗	⊗	⊗	⊗	●	⊗
University of Texas (Austin)	⊗	●	●	●	◒	●	◒	⊗	●	⊗
University of Virginia	⊗	⊗	●	●	⊗	⊗	⊗	⊗	●	⊗

Community Involvement							Other
Teen Programs	Demonstration Projects	Co-operation w/ other Groups	Involvement in Local Projects	Site Tours Available	Conference Sponsorship	Spiritual Framework	
⊗	⊗	◓	◓	◓	●	⊗	
◓	●	●	●	●	◓	⊗	Brownfield Remediation; Environmental Justice
⊗	●	●	●	●	●	⊗	
⊗	●	●	●	●	◓	⊗	Building Investment Decision Support; Systems Integration
⊗	◓	⊗	●	◓	⊗	⊗	Culture & Sustainability; Community Service-Learning
⊗	●	●	●	●	●	⊗	
⊗	●	●	●	●	◓	◓	Social Justice
⊗	⊗	●	●	●	●	⊗	Organic Design; Ecological Project Management
⊗	⊗	◓	◓	⊗	⊗	⊗	
⊗	●	⊗	⊗	⊗	⊗	⊗	
⊗	⊗	●	●	●	●	⊗	Design for Deconstruction; Reused Material Certification
⊗	●	●	●	◓	◓	⊗	
●	●	●	●	●	●	⊗	
◓	◓	◓	◓	◓	◓	⊗	
⊗	◓	◓	◓	◓	●	⊗	
⊗	⊗	⊗	●	⊗	●	⊗	Green Modular Construction; Design Discipline Integration

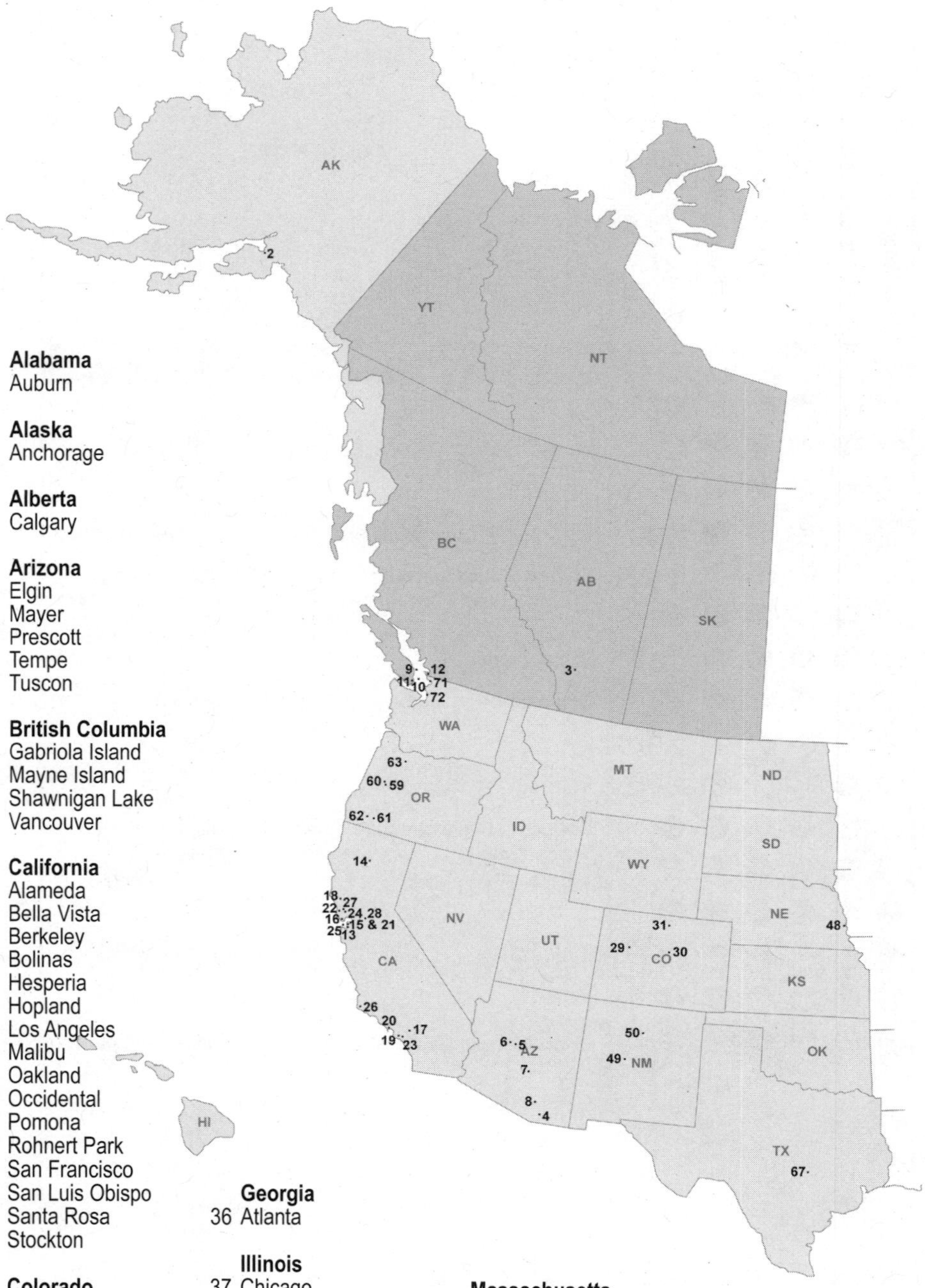

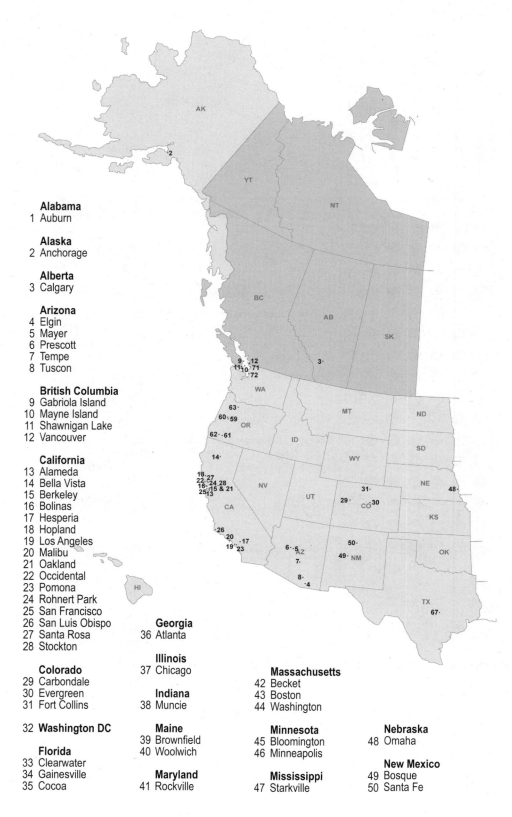

Alabama
1 Auburn

Alaska
2 Anchorage

Alberta
3 Calgary

Arizona
4 Elgin
5 Mayer
6 Prescott
7 Tempe
8 Tuscon

British Columbia
9 Gabriola Island
10 Mayne Island
11 Shawnigan Lake
12 Vancouver

California
13 Alameda
14 Bella Vista
15 Berkeley
16 Bolinas
17 Hesperia
18 Hopland
19 Los Angeles
20 Malibu
21 Oakland
22 Occidental
23 Pomona
24 Rohnert Park
25 San Francisco
26 San Luis Obispo
27 Santa Rosa
28 Stockton

Colorado
29 Carbondale
30 Evergreen
31 Fort Collins

32 **Washington DC**

Florida
33 Clearwater
34 Gainesville
35 Cocoa

Georgia
36 Atlanta

Illinois
37 Chicago

Indiana
38 Muncie

Maine
39 Brownfield
40 Woolwich

Maryland
41 Rockville

Massachusetts
42 Becket
43 Boston
44 Washington

Minnesota
45 Bloomington
46 Minneapolis

Mississippi
47 Starkville

Nebraska
48 Omaha

New Mexico
49 Bosque
50 Santa Fe

United States and Canada School Locations

Alphabetical by State/Province

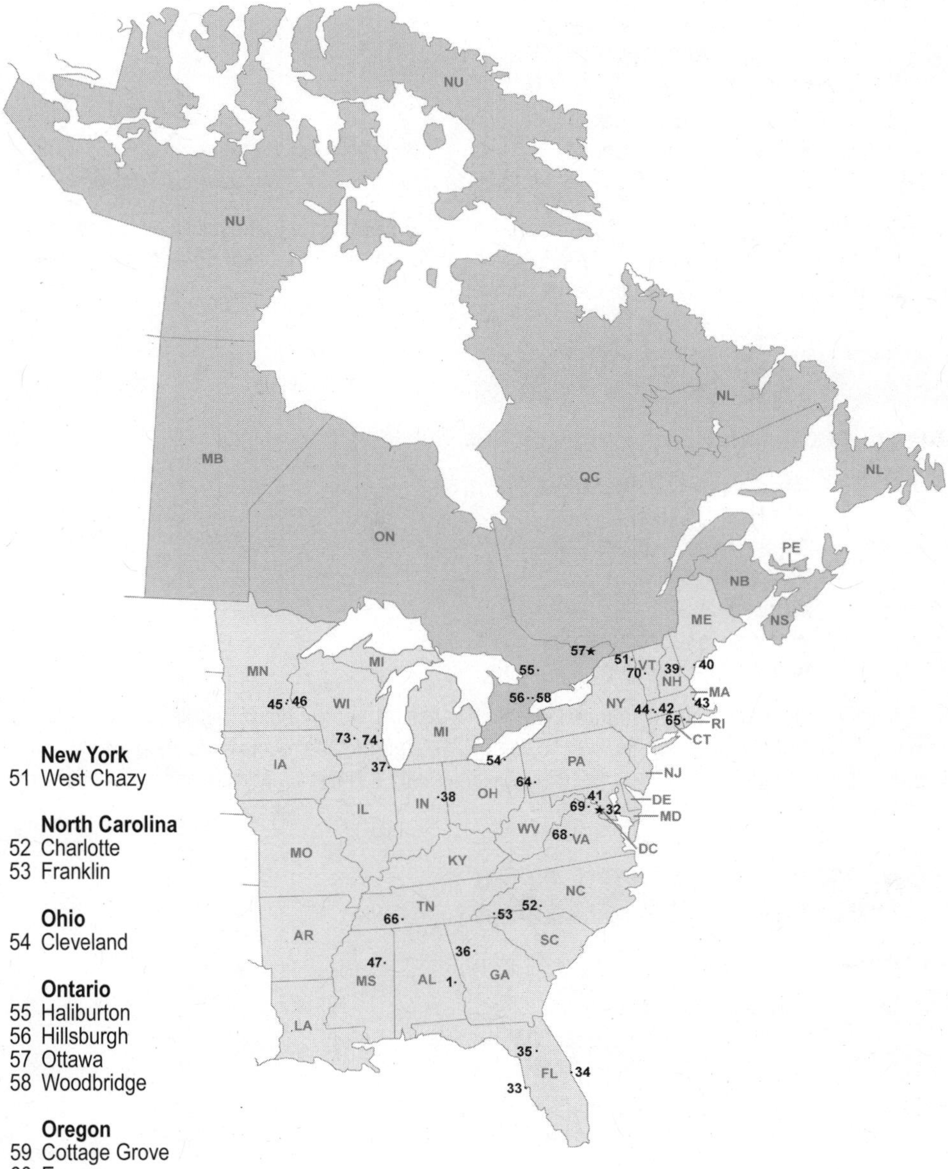

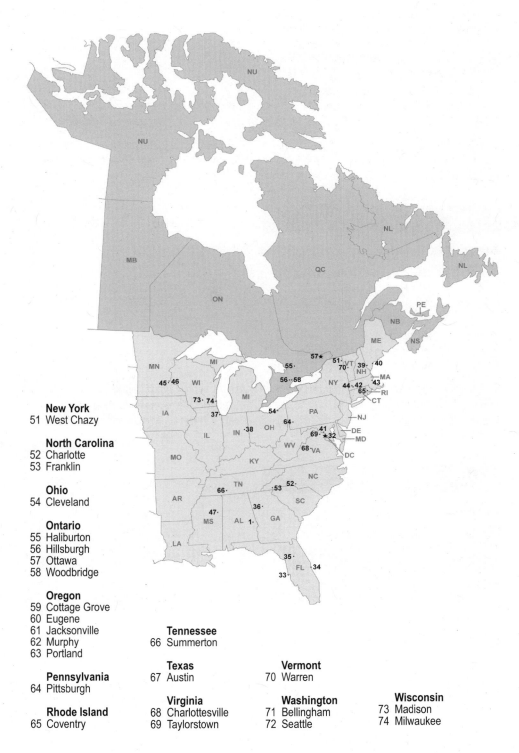

New York
51 West Chazy

North Carolina
52 Charlotte
53 Franklin

Ohio
54 Cleveland

Ontario
55 Haliburton
56 Hillsburgh
57 Ottawa
58 Woodbridge

Oregon
59 Cottage Grove
60 Eugene
61 Jacksonville
62 Murphy
63 Portland

Pennsylvania
64 Pittsburgh

Rhode Island
65 Coventry

Tennessee
66 Summerton

Texas
67 Austin

Virginia
68 Charlottesville
69 Taylorstown

Vermont
70 Warren

Washington
71 Bellingham
72 Seattle

Wisconsin
73 Madison
74 Milwaukee

Alabama

Auburn University

higher education

Contact Bruce Lindsey, *Co-Director*
Rural Studio School of Architecture
202 Dudley Commons
Auburn, AL 36849
334-844-5426
rstudio@auburn.edu
Website www.ruralstudio.com
Periodical *Rural Studio: Samuel Mockbee and the Architecture of Decency*

The Rural Studio is an innovative program based on the concept of "context-based learning," wherein students take up residency in poverty-stricken Hale County, Alabama, and other communities to design and build housing for actual clients in need.

Alaska

Alaska Craftsman Home Program, Inc.

professional continuing education

Contact Chuck Renfro, *Vice President*
PO Box 241647
Anchorage, AK 99524
907-258-2247
achp@alaska.net
Website www.alaska.net/~achp/
Periodical *Northern Comfort*

The Alaska Craftsmen Home Program has been teaching energy efficient building concepts to builders and homeowners for more than 15 years. The program has received national awards, and is recognized as highly effective in assisting builders with licensing qualifications and continuing education needs.

Alberta

University of Calgary

higher education

Contact Melody Wenet
2500 University Drive NW
Calgary, AB T2N 1N4
403-220-6601
info@evds.ucalgary.ca
Website www.ucalgary.ca/evds

We live in the world by design. Design asks us to find answers to the most fundamental of human questions: how should we live in the world and what should inform our actions? Creating the everyday environment in which we live involves cultural meaning, visual communication, and technology. Environmental Design focuses on interdisciplinary physical and social interventions in the built, natural, and human environments, informed by human behavior and environmental processes.

Arizona State University

higher education

Contact Harvey Bryan
School of Architecture
Arizona State University
Tempe, AZ 85287
480-965-3536
arch.grad@asu.edu
Website www.asu.edu/caed/sala/index.htm

Architecture and related departments including a strong building science emphasis and a program in Energy Performance and Climate-Responsive Architecture.

....

Arcosanti

continuing education | hands-on

Contact Kelli Huth, *Workshop Coordinator*
HC 74, Box 4136
Mayer, AZ 86333
928-632-6233
workshop@arcosanti.org
Website www.arcosanti.org
Periodical *Arcommunique*

Arcosanti is an educational process. The five week workshop program teaches building techniques and arcological philosophy, while continuing the city's construction. Volunteers and students come from around the world. Many are design students, and some receive university credit for the workshop, but a design or architecture background is not necessary. People of many varied interests and backgrounds are all contributing their valuable time and skills to the project. Week-long silt sculpture workshops and Elderhostel programs offer other ways to be involved. At the present stage of construction, Arcosanti consists of various mixed-use buildings and public spaces constructed by over 5000 past workshop participants.

....

Canelo Project

continuing education | hands-on

Contact Bill & Athena Steen, *Co-founders*
HC 1, Box 324
Elgin, AZ 85611
520-455-5548
absteen@dakotacom.net
Website www.caneloproject.com
Periodical *The Straw Bale House; The Beauty of Straw Bale Homes*

The Canelo Project is a small non-profit organization dedicated to the education, research, and development of sustainable living practices that encourage beauty and simplicity. The Project offers on-going workshops, internships, and consulting in straw bale and straw-clay block construction, clay-lime plasters and floors, natural paints, earthen baking ovens and low-cost housing in the U.S. and Mexico. In addition, the organization hosts a bed and breakfast and offers site tours.

DAWN Southwest

Contact J. Joyce, *Owner*
6570 West Illinois Street
Tucson, AZ 85735
520-624-1673
dawnaz@earthlink.net
Website www.greenbuilder.com/dawn

DAWN Southwest (formerly Out On Bale By Mail) is a demonstration site for natural building and sustainable living. Owner, Joelee Joyce, welcomes visitors to come and spend a day playing with cob, earthen plasters, and clay paints, or water harvesting and land restoration. Join a workshop and experience the joys of creating small, natural buildings that reflect the owner/builder's touch in appearance and form. Support from partners and friends makes it possible to realize the vision of building relationships and weaving connections to the earth. DAWN-Developing Alliances with Nature. The organization offers opportunities to exchange work for workshop participation.

Ecosa Institute

Contact Antony Brown, *Director*
212B South Marina Street
Prescott, AZ 86303
928-541-1002
info@ecosainstitute.org
Website www.ecosainstitute.org
Periodical *Design Matters*

The Ecosa Institute, located in Prescott, Arizona, is a non-profit organization offering semester long immersion programs in sustainable design for undergraduates, graduates, and professionals. Participants learn the impact that design has on the natural and built environment and are exposed to alternative strategies for reducing that impact. Students travel to ancient and modern sites around Arizona, meet with nationally recognized leaders in the field, and work on real projects with real clients to provide design solutions.

British Columbia

Cobworks

Contact Patrick Henneberry
RP 1
Mayne Island, BC V0N 2T0
250-539-5253
pat@cobworks.com
Website www.cobworks.com

Cobworks is committed to building beautiful, affordable structures with natural and local material in a spirit of cooperation and social responsibility. All workshops provide an exciting opportunity to learn through hands-on practice, presentations, teamwork, and the fun of working as a group.

Island School of Building Arts

professional | continuing education | hands-on

Contact Kathleen Lasby, *Programs Coordinat*
3199 Coast Road
Gabriola Island, BC V0R 1X7
250-247-8922
info@logandtimberschool.com
Website www.logandtimberschool.com
Periodical *The Craft of Modular Post and Beam*

Located on the beautiful, pristine Gulf Island of Gabriola, just a short ferry ride or flight from picturesque Vancouver BC. Established in 1997, ISBA is the only bonded, Registered Trade School (PPSEC #2387) in British Columbia, Canada, specializing in teaching Log and Timber Frame Construction Skills for Industry Pre Employment.

....

One United Resource Ecovillage

continuing education | hands-on

Contact Brandy Gallagher-MacPherson
PO Box 530
Shawnigan Lake, BC V0R 2W0
250-743-3067
our@pacificcoast.net
Website www.ourecovillage.org
Periodical *OUR News; Creating Topia*

O.U.R. Ecovillage is a 25-acre demonstration sustainable village. The lifestyle is intergenerational, intercultural, and interfaith. The space offers residents and visitors a bridge between the seeming dichotomies of life: rural/urban, individual/group. O.U.R Ecovillage offers a wide range of programs from a summer school ("Plan B") to workshops on strawbale and cob construction.

....

University of British Columbia

higher education

Contact Trish Poehnel
6333 Memorial Road
Suite 402
Vancouver, BC V6T 1Z2
604-822-2779
tpoehnel@interchange.ubc.ca
Website www.arch.ubc.ca

The School of Architecture at the University of British Columbia offers a graduate level professional and post-professional degree. One key research concern is the investigation of environmentally responsible design and building practice.

California

Building Education Center

Contact Sydney Adams
812 Page Street
Berkeley, CA 94710
510-525-7610
syd@bldgeductr.org
Website www.bldgeductr.org
Periodical *Earthquake Retrofitting; Class Schedule*

The Building Education Center is a California non-profit corporation based in West Berkeley, California since 1992. The BEC offers approximately 60 different classes and workshops for consumers, homeowners, beginning tradespeople, those in career transition and professionals seeking to broaden their construction skills through short practical coursework.

Cal-Earth Institute / Geltaftan Foundation

Contact Iliona Outram
10376 Shangri-La Avenue
Hesperia, CA 92345
760-244-0614
calearth@aol.com
Website www.calearth.org

The California Institute of Earth Art and Architecture is at the cutting edge of Earth (superadobe) and Ceramic Architecture technologies today. Cal-Earth was founded by architect and author Nader Khalili to promote research and education of the public into the equilibrium of the universal elements of Earth, Water, Air, and Fire, and their unity in the service of the environment and humanity. Its scope spans technical innovations published by NASA to United Nations endorsed housing for the world's homeless.

California Polytechnic State University at Pomona
John T. Lyle Center for Regenerative Studies

Contact Dr. Kyle Brown, *Director*
4105 West University Drive
Pomona, CA 91768
909-869-5155
crs@csupomona.edu
Website www.csupomona.edu/~crs/index.html

The mission of the John T. Lyle Center for Regenerative Studies is to advance the principles of environmentally sustainable living through education, research, demonstration and community outreach. It offers unique interdisciplinary education through its Master of Science degree program, its undergraduate minor program, and community workshops that prepare students to integrate regenerative theories and practices into a wide variety of professional fields and projects. Students have the option of residing and/or working at the Center.

California Polytechnic State University (San Luis Obispo)

higher education

Contact Robert Peña
One Grand Avenue
San Luis Obispo, CA 93407
805-756-1316
architecture@calpoly.edu
Website www.caed.calpoly.edu/arch.html

While holistic in scope, the Cal Poly SLO architecture program offers areas of special focus, culminating in an exit-year project. One such area of focus is the "Sustainable Environments" minor, offered to students throughout the University. Cal Poly's "learning-by-doing" educational approach is realized through both the design studio curriculum and regular college events such as Design Village, an annual design-build competition that takes place in the outdoor rural "laboratory" of Poly Canyon. Student teams from around the country construct and inhabit small, prefabricated dwellings for a weekend.

....

Kupono Natural Builders

continuing education

hands-on

Contact Jonathon Freeman & Miki'ala Catalfa, *Founders*
PO Box 828
Bella Vista, CA 96008
530-275-3623
kuponobuilders@snowcrest.net
Website www.kuponobuilders.com

Kupono Natural Builders serve Northern California communities around Redding, hosting natural building workshops. Workshop participants learn basic building skills which focus on earthen buildings, including cob, cob/strawbale hybrids, earth bags, recycled materials, and passive solar design, while being immersed in a respectful and sustainable lifestyle. "Malia paha he iki 'unu, pa'a ka pohaku nui 'a'ole e ka'a" (Perhaps it is the small stone that can keep the big rock from rolling down.) -- Hawaiian proverb

....

Laney College

Green Carpentry Program

professional

Contact Cynthia Correia, *Program Director*
900 Fallon Street
Oakland, CA 94607
510-451-2617
Website www.peralta.cc.ca.us/laney

Laney College has incorporated a program into its vocational Department of Carpentry that provide students hands-on experience building green affordable housing in the local community.

Merritt College

Ecological Design and Energy Technology Program

Contact Robin Mark Freeman, *Chair*
12500 Camus Drive
Oakland, CA 94619
510-434-3840
ecomerritt@sbcglobal.net
Website www.merritt.edu
Periodical *Introduction to Green Building*

Merritt is a community college in the Oakland Hills above San Francisco Bay. It has offered an introductory, hands-on Green Building program in the student-and-faculty-built center since 1980. Some advanced and public workshops are also available.

New College of California

EcoDwelling Concentration

Contact Joseph F. Kennedy, *Program Coordinator*
99 6th Street
Santa Rosa, CA 95404
707-568-3092
jkennedy@newcollege.edu
Website www.ecodwelling.org
Periodical *The Art of Natural Building; Building Without Borders*

The EcoDwelling concentration of New College of California (part of BA completion or MA degree) is a holistic approach to design and construction concerned with the causes of dwelling failure and the design of equitable, sustainable, universally affordable alternatives. Through lecture, discussion, design projects, and hands-on building, this concentration encourages students to develop their vision of sustainable design using natural materials and ecological processes.

Occidental Arts and Ecology Center

Contact Philip Tymon, *Administrative Director*
15290 Coleman Valley Road
Occidental, CA 95465
707-874-1557
oaec@oaec.org
Website www.oaec.org
Periodical Catalog

The Occidental Arts and Ecology Center offers the following courses relevant to Natural Building and Carpentry: Natural Paints, Plasters, and Pigments; Carpentry for Women; Green Building Tours; Permaculture Design; Sustainable Forestry; Stormwater Management. Other building courses are created when projects on Center land arise. There is also a maintenance internship offered which includes carpentry and sometimes natural building.

Pacific Gas & Electric's Pacific Energy Center

Contact Beverly Coleman
851 Howard Street
San Francisco, CA 94103
415-973-2277
pecinfo@pge.com
Website www.pge.com/pec
Periodical *E-Zine: The PEC Electronic Magazine*

Since 1991 the Pacific Energy Center has provided architectural and engineering professionals with 100 classes per year, design tools, and advice to create energy-efficient environments while assuring high levels of occupant well being and building value. The services, provided free of charge, include assistance in: daylighting/shading analysis of building models to optimize envelope design; architectural consultations on site orientation, glazing, daylighting, and electric lighting; electric lighting system demonstrations; and tool lending library services for measuring building performance.

Pacific Gas & Electric's Stockton Energy Training Center

Contact Charles F. Segerstrom
1129 Enterprise Street
Stockton, CA 95204
209-932-2500
Website www.pge.com/stockton
Periodical Course Calendar

The Energy Training Center is a unique facility offering continuing education to residential contractors, building inspectors, architects, engineers, and home designers. Hands-on instruction covers the proper use, installation, maintenance, and testing of energy-efficient windows, insulation materials, as well as heating, ventilation, and air conditioning (HVAC) systems. Implementation of energy-efficient measures and practices is the emphasis in every class. The "house as a system" approach is stressed, and students learn by working on residential mock-ups.

San Francisco Institute of Architecture

Contact Fred A. Stitt, *Director*
PO Box 2590
Alameda, CA 94501
510-523-5174
sfia@aol.com
Website www.sfia.net

The nation's first and most comprehensive Eco-Design programs, including Distance Learning and Continuing Education. SFIA is devoted to innovation, and reform in architectural education, offering open classes and a Master of Architecture program to graduate students, architectural employees, practicing professionals, and those who have yet to start their architectural education. Working students appreciate that classes are scheduled evenings or Saturdays.

Seven Generations Natural Builders

Contact Tim Reith, *Co-founder*
SBGN Attn: Sasha Rabin
PO Box 735
Bolinas, CA 94924
415-310-7460
tim@sgnb.com
Website www.sgnb.com

Seven Generations Natural Builders provides teaching, consultation/design, and construction services using cob, straw, wood, and stone. Emphasis is placed on using local materials and the integration of the vernacular architecture of a region into contemporary building. Workshops offer hands-on experience in siting and design, building with natural and recycled materials, materials prospecting, testing, and procurement, passive solar design, roofs, earthen floors, and natural plasters. SGNB is dedicated to teaching people how to house themselves.

....

Solar Living Institute

Contact Bob Gragson
PO Box 836
Hopland, CA 95449
707-744-2100
sli@solarliving.org
Website www.solarliving.org
Periodical *Real Good News*

Since 1992, over 3,500 students have attended Solar Living Institute hands-on workshops on renewable energy, ecological design, sustainable living, and alternative construction techniques like strawbale, cob, and bamboo. Over half a million people have visited the 12-acre Solar Living Center where it is situated in Hopland, California. The Center is powered entirely by renewable energy systems, and features a 5,000 sq. foot, passive-solar, strawbale building. Visitors enjoy interactive displays and an extensive Permaculture landscape with organically grown edible and ornamental plants. Special programs include the annual Solfest, Northern California's premier summer environmental festival, and a year-round, intensive Intern Program.

....

Sonoma State University
Environmental Technology Center

Contact Armando Navarro, *Operations Manager*
1801 East Cotati Avenue
Rohnert Park, CA 94928
707-664-2577
armando.navarro@sonoma.edu
Website www.sonoma.edu/ensp/etc

Sonoma State's year-long "Green Building Professional Certification Program" is designed to give working professionals the understanding necessary to make sustainable building decisions within a corporate, institutional, non-profit, municipal or individual setting. The program consists of: 1) Green Building Overview; 2) Site Selection/Design and Water-Efficient Practices; 3) Energy Sources, End Uses and Impacts; 4) Green Building Material; 5) Indoor Environmental Quality; and 6) Innovative Green Building Case Studies. Students must also complete an independent study project.

University of California at Berkeley

Contact Edward Arens, *CEDR Director*
Department of Architecture
232 Wurster Hall - MC#1800
Berkeley, CA 94720
510-642-4942
earens@uclink.berkeley.edu
Website http://arch.ced.berkeley.edu

UC Berkeley's College of Environmental Design has been home to a number of ecologically-oriented faculty and students over time. It's strong emphasis in building science is anchored in the Building Science Laboratory, operations include Green Architecture Research and Design partnership with the University of California Energy Institute (UCEI), the Center for Environmental Design Research (CEDR), and the College is home to the Vital Signs Project. Student groups include Green Architecture Research and Design (GARD) and Students for Environmental Architecture (SEArch).

....

University of Southern California

Contact Dr. Douglas Noble, *Associate Professor*
Watt Hall 204
Los Angeles, CA 90089
213-740-4589
dnoble@usc.edu
Website www.usc.edu/dept/architecture

The USC School of Architecture is committed to environmental sustainability. Research focuses on both new science and engineering developments for high-performance building systems, design guidelines and decision support tools, as well as demonstration projects. The Masters of Building Science lab encourages the use of renewable materials and construction systems, and renewable energy, through appropriate, advanced climate and occupant-based technology, and the promotion of solar low-energy and passive solar systems. The lab also focuses on the life cycle and recyclability of targeted building materials. Urban Los Angeles serves as a stimulating laboratory, itself, for the study of sustainability, social and cultural responsibility, and for forming alliances in global, regional, and local green networks.

....

Wright Way Organic Resource Center

Contact Peg Butler, *Assistant Director*
24680 Piuma Road
Malibu, CA 90265
818-591-8992
wworc@elwright.net
Website www.elwright.net/wrightway
Periodical *Wright News*

Wright Way Organic Resource Center melds the practices and principles of Organic Architecture, ecological responsibility, and social equity to promote positive ways for people to engage with their environments and communities. Through educational programs, workshop experiences, community celebrations, resource center facilities and outreach, the Center strives to provide opportunities for the diverse Los Angeles population, especially inner-city youth, to expand their skills and visions for the present and future.

Colorado

Colorado State University at Fort Collins
Institute for the Sustainable Built Environment

higher education · professional

Contact Brian Dunbar, *Director*
Guggenheim Hall
Fort Collins, CO 80523-1584
970-491-5041
dunbar@cahs.colostate.edu
Website www.ibe.colostate.edu

The Institute for the Built Environment (IBE), housed in the Construction Management Department at Colorado State University, is an energetic interdisciplinary center for environmentally-responsible building design and construction. In addition to a graduate emphasis, IBE offers an evening course for professionals and a 2-week intensive in St. John, U.S. Virgin Islands. IBE customizes trainings, design charrettes, and research projects, is a member of the US Green Building Council, and a founding member of the USGBC-Colorado Chapter.

Eco-Broker

professional

Contact Dr. John Beldock
29029 Upper Bear Creek Road
Suite 202
Evergreen, CO 80439
800-706-4321
customerservice@ecobroker.com
Website www.ecobroker.com

EcoBroker is an education and market performance program designed exclusively for real estate professionals and industry affiliates, including an EcoBroker Certification program with three courses in its curriculum: EcoBroker Environmental Advantage(TM), EcoBroker Energy Advantage(TM), and EcoBroker Green Market Advantage(TM).

Rocky Mountain Workshops

continuing education · hands-on

Contact Peter Haney, *Founder*
505 N. Grant Avenue
Fort Collins, CO 80521
970-482-1366
peter@rockymountainworkshops.com
Website www.rockymountainworkshops.com

Offering hands-on workshops in traditional building techniques since 1986, including round log and timber frame joinery, design, and scribed and compound joinery. Rocky Mountain Workshops received sponsorship from the Timber Framers Guild in 1996.

Solar Energy International

professional · continuing education · hands-on

Contact	Rachel Ware 76 S. 2nd Street Carbondale, CO 81623 970-963-8855 sei@solarenergy.org
Website	www.solarenergy.org
Periodical	*SEI Journal; Photovoltaic Design and Installation Manual*

Solar Energy International (SEI) is a nonprofit organization promoting renewable energy and environmental building technologies through education and technical assistance. SEI serves decision makers, technicians, and users of renewable energy sources. SEI also provides the expertise to plan, engineer, and implement sustainable development projects.

District of Columbia

Shaw EcoVillage

continuing education · hands-on

Contact	Noel F. Petrie 1701 6th Street NW Washington, DC 20010 202-265-2019 sev.noelpetrie@verizon.net
Website	www.shawecovillage.com
Periodical	Annual Report; Newsletter

The Shaw EcoVillage Project trains at-risk youth to be catalysts for sustainable change in Washington, D.C. neighborhoods. SEV's oldest program, the EcoDesign Corps, is a paid internship for high-schools students in which teams of interns work to address a particular problem affecting the community. EDC interns provide expertise on smart growth, environmental stewardship, and equitable development.

U.S. Green Building Council

professional · continuing education

Contact	Ana L. Kaahanui 1015 18th Street NW Suite 508 Washington, DC 20036 workshop@usgbc.org
Website	www.usgbc.org

The U.S. Green Building Council (USGBC) is the nation's leading nonprofit coalition for advancing buildings that are environmentally responsible, profitable and healthy places to live and work. Major programs supporting its mission include the Council's Leadership in Energy and Environmental Design (LEED®) Green Building Rating System; LEED Workshops; LEED Professional Accreditation; the Greenbuild International Conference & Expo; and a robust local chapter program.

Florida

International Institute for Bau-biologie and Ecology, Inc.

Contact Helmut Ziehe, *Founder*
1401-A Cleveland Street
Clearwater, FL 33755
baubiologie@earthlink.net
Website www.buildingbiology.net

professional continuing education

IBE, a non-profit educational organization, offers programs in the field of Bau-biologie also known as Building Biology. This interdisciplinary study focuses on the impact buildings have on health and well-being as well as on the ecological situation. Topics include electromagnetic radiation, indoor air, water, and building materials. For new and remodel structures, solutions are identified through the use of thoughtful design and construction methods combined with healthy building materials. Study programs include Online Study, Certification, Homeowner Course, Workshops, and Seminars. Also available: consulting, literature, and instruments.

Florida Solar Energy Center

Contact Robin Vierra
1679 Clearlake Road
Cocoa, FL 32922
321-638-1015
info@fsec.ucf.edu
Website www.fsec.ucf.edu

professional

FSEC has been a leader in renewable energy and energy efficiency research and training for over 20 years. It is currently the largest state-supported research and training institute in the U.S. in the area of renewable energy and building energy efficiency. FSEC has nearly a hundred professionals on staff with expertise in engineering, energy research, building science, energy and policy analysis and education and training. Ongoing, one- and two-day courses are offered for continuing education units (CEUs) on such subjects as photovoltaics, home energy rating certification, energy-efficient building strategies, and alternative fuel vehicles.

University of Florida
Powell Center for Construction & Environment

Contact Dr. Charles J. Kibert, *Director*
University of Florida
PO Box 115703
Gainesville, FL 32611-5703
352-273-1189
ckibert@ufl.edu
Website www.cce.ufl.edu

higher education professional

The Powell Center for Construction and Environment is a research center whose mission is to foster the incorporation of sustainability into the built environment sector of the economy. The Powell Center also conducts courses for graduate programs at the University of Florida, assists in the development of green building standards, coordinates international and national green building research efforts, and provides support for community sustainability efforts.

Georgia

Southface Energy Institute

professional · continuing education

Contact Abigail Paine, *Communications Coordinator*
241 Pine Street NE
Atlanta, GA 30308
404-872-3549
info@southface.org
Website www.southface.org
Periodical *Southface Journal of Sustainable Building*

Southface Energy Institute is nationally recognized for work in energy efficiency, building science, and environmental sustainability. Established as a non-profit in 1978, Southface promotes sustainable homes, workplaces, and communities through education, research, advocacy, and technical assistance. Since 1996, Southface has been headquartered in the Southface Energy and Environmental Resource Center, a demonstration house with more than 100 energy-efficient and environmentally-sound products, technologies, and building practices.

Illinois

Chicago Center for Green Technology

professional

Contact Elise Zelechowski
445 N. Sacramento Boulevard
Chicago, IL 60612
312-746-9642
greentech@cityofchicago.org
Website www.cityofchicago.org/Environment/GreenTech

Chicago Green Tech offers a dynamic green building educational program that is free and open to the public. Chicago Green Tech also houses the Green Building Resource Center which offers a wide variety of green building reference media including books, periodicals, sample building materials, computer software, LEED guides and more.

Indiana

Ball State University

Center for Energy Research/Education/Service

higher education

Contact Robert J. Koester, *Director*
2000 University Avenue
Suite AB018
Muncie, IN 47306-0170
765-285-1135
rkoester@bsu.edu
Website www.bsu.edu/ceres
Periodical *Greening of the Campus*

The Center for Energy Research/Education/Service (CERES) at Ball State University, Muncie, is an interdisciplinary academic support unit focused on issues related to energy and resource conservation. The Center serves the campus, local, state and regional communities through ongoing examination of state-of-the-art energy conservation and end-use practices. Innovative academic offerings include Clustered Minors in Environmentally Sustainable Practices, the Vital Signs Course, and the Graduate Studio in Sustainable Design offered as part of a post-professional degree program in the Department of Architecture.

Maine

Fox Maple School of Traditional Building

continuing education · hands-on

Contact Steve Chappell
PO Box 249
Brownfield, ME 04010
207-935-3720
foxmaple@foxmaple.com
Website www.foxmaple.com
Periodical *Joiners' Quarterly; A Timber Framer's Workshop*

Fox Maple provides the opportunity for people to learn traditional timber framing and natural building skills in a rural campus setting, The campus is a learning center, a work in progress, crafted by students. Workshops begin with a joined timber frame, and then explore the use of natural enclosures; thatch, straw/clay, wood chip/clay, wattle & daub, cob, straw bales, finished with earth plasters. Fine craftsmanship lies at the heart of Fox Maple's teaching philosophy. Its traveling workshops offer the same approach to people in diverse locations throughout the U.S and the world.

....

Shelter Institute

continuing education · hands-on

Contact Patsy Hennin, *Co-Founder*
873 Route One
Woolwich, ME 04579
207-442-7938
info@shelterinstitute.com
Website www.shelterinstitute.com
Periodical *Info to Build On*

Program of hands-on, owner-builder courses emphasizing timber-framing, super-efficient construction and small house design.

Maryland

Montgomery College

continuing education

Contact Randy Steiner
51 Mannakee Street
Rockville, MD 20850
301-251-7599
randy.steiner@montgomerycollege.edu
Website www.montgomerycollege.edu/architecture

Montgomery College's one-credit classes were developed to offer students a glimpse into the impact of energy conservation on the built environment. The first class, Principles of Sustainability and Green Architecture, is an introduction to the ecology issues of construction and design. The second class, The Technology of Energy Conservation, covers energy resources and the various means of reducing waste. The last class, Advanced Studies in Energy Conservation, focuses on specific applications of green design to individual buildings.

Boston Architectural Center

Sustainable Design Certificate Program

professional

Contact: Maia B. Nilsson, *Director of Certificate Programs*
320 Newbury Street
Boston, MA 02115
617-585-0101
ce@the-bac.edu
Website: www.the-bac.edu/ce

Architects and interior designers are increasingly challenged to design places in harmony with the environment. The BAC's Certificate in Sustainable Design prepares practitioners to meet this challenge through courses that address how to make wise use of natural resources, minimize energy use, reduce waste, and preserve biosystems. Founded over 110 years ago as an architectural club, the BAC today is New England's largest independent professional college of architecture and interior design.

....

Heartwood School for the Homebuilding Crafts

continuing education | hands-on

Contact: Will Beemer, *Programs Director*
Johnson Hill Road
Washington, MA 01223
413-623-6677
willb@heartwoodschool.com
Website: www.heartwoodschool.com
Periodical: Annual Brochure

The Heartwood School was established in 1978 to teach the skills and knowledge it takes to build an energy-efficient house. Since that time, program offerings have expanded to include all aspects of the homebuilding crafts, particularly timber framing. The School offers one- to-three-week courses (hands-on) in energy efficient homebuilding, timber framing, and woodworking.

....

Timber Framers Guild

professional | continuing education | hands-on

Contact: Will Beemer, *Executive Director*
PO Box 60
Becket, MA 01223
888-453-0879
info@tfguild.org
Website: www.tfguild.org
Periodical: *Timber Framing; Scantlings*

The Timber Framers Guild is a non-profit educational membership association open to all who are interested in the trade and craft of timber framing. The Guild hosts conferences, publish and distribute training materials, teach workshops, and organize community service building projects around the world.

Minnesota

Energy and Environmental Building Association
Institute of Building Construction Technology

professional

Contact	Kathleen Guidera, *Executive Director* 10740 Lyndale Avenue S Suite 10-W Bloomington, MN 55420 952-881-1098 eebainfo@eeba.org
Website	www.eeba.org/institute
Periodical	*EEBA Builder's Guide*

EEBA promotes the awareness, education and development of energy efficient, as well as environmentally responsible, buildings and communities. EEBA has developed new building technology, created standards for energy efficiency, and established best field practices and their applications. The Institute of Building Technology uses the "Systems Approach" to building to deliver the very latest research and technology through education courses and annual conferences.

University of Minnesota
Center for Sustainable Building Research

higher education

Contact	John Carmody, *Director* 1425 University Avenue SE Suite 115 Minneapolis, MN 55455 csbr@umn.edu
Website	www.csbr.umn.edu

The Center for Sustainable Building Research (CSBR) is a place for organizing and effectively growing the research and outreach missions of the College of Architecture and Landscape Architecture (CALA). CSBR works with other units to enhance CALA's teaching mission and serves as a resource for the State of Minnesota, the design professions, and the building industry.

Mississippi

Mississippi State University
Center for Sustainable Design

higher education

Contact	Pete Melby, *Co-Director* PO Box 9725 Mississippi State University Starkville, MS 39762 pm@ra.msstate.edu
Website	www.abe.msstate.edu/csd/

The Center for Sustainable Design (CSD) was created by Pete Melby, Professor of Landscape Architecture, and Tom Cathcart, Professor of Biological Engineering, who shared an interest in the use of natural (i.e., biological) approaches to solve man-made problems. Due to this common interest, almost all of their class projects required the use of sustainable systems in their solutions. The CSD was officially formed within the Water Resources Research Institute.

Nebraska

Joslyn Castle Institute for Sustainable Communities

professional | continuing education

Contact Christine Dahlin, *Director of Communications*
3902 Davenport Street
Omaha, NE 68131
402-595-1902
ccdahlin@sustainabledesign.org
Website www.ecospheres.com

Founded in 1996, the Joslyn Castle Institute for Sustainable Communities focuses on the built environment to promote sustainable development. A community development organization, they encourage the efficient use of resources. Through education, research, and outreach, JCI seeks to improve the capacity of communities to address issues of environmental concern with economic and social development. On behalf of the State of Nebraska, the Institute manages daily operation of the historic Joslyn Castle estate.

New Mexico

EcoVersity

professional | continuing education | hands-on

Contact Arina Pittman, *Managing Director*
2639 Agua Fria
Santa Fe, NM 87505
505-424-9797
info@ecoversity.org
Website www.ecoversity.org
Periodical Catalog

Courses at the EcoVersity provide practical ways to learn land skills and sharpen visions for a sustainable future. EcoVersity continuing education courses are specifically designed for the climate and conditions of New Mexico. EcoVersity's hallmark is hands-on experiential learning leading to real world problem solving. B499Students are trained to expand their observation skills, awareness and appreciation of the natural world.

Southwest Solar Adobe School

continuing education

Contact Joe Tibbets
PO Box 153
Bosque, NM 87006
505-861-2287
adobebuilder@juno.com
Website www.adobebuilder.com
Periodical *Adobe Builder; Earthbuilders' Encyclopedia*

Twenty-five years ago, Southwest Solaradobe (SWSA) began classes in adobe construction in New Mexico. Since that time, SWSA has conducted classes throughout the Southwest, adding Texas, Arizona, California, and Colorado to the states where classes have been offered. SWSA has also supported USAID with adobe building programs in rural areas of Honduras, and delivered earth building presentations at the University of Costa Rica in San José. SWSA has helped in developing earth building codes to protect the right of contractors and owner-builders to permit and build. The organization is a member of ASTM and works on adoption of new building codes. SWSA also publishes Adobe Builder, a publication about earthbuilding.

New York

Earthwood Building School

Contact Rob Roy, *Co-Founder*
366 Murtagh Hill Road
West Chazy, NY 12992
518-493-7744
robandjaki@yahoo.com
Website www.cordwoodmasonry.com
Periodical *Club Meg News: The Journal for Stone Circle Builders*

Earthwood Building School, founded in 1981, conducts hands-on workshops in cordwood masonry construction and megalithic (stone circle) building, as well as classroom instruction in earth-sheltered housing and earth roofs. Most workshops are held at the Earthwood campus near West Chazy in northern New York, May through September; regional workshops are conducted throughout North America and overseas. Earthwood also serves as a clearinghouse for books, plans, and videos on their courses of study and related subject matter.

North Carolina

Goshen Timber Frames

Contact Cathy Bryan
37 Phillips Street
Franklin, NC 28734
828-524-8662
info@goshenframes.com
Website www.goshenframes.com
Periodical *www.timberframemag.com*

Goshen Timber Frames hosts weeklong workshops taught by professional joiners and has year round apprenticeships for those interested in learning the craft of timber framing. Please be advised that space is limited, so plan accordingly.

University of North Carolina at Charlotte

Contact Kenneth Lambla, *Dean*
9201 University City Boulevard
Charlotte, NC 28223-0001
704-687-4841
kalambla@email.uncc.edu
Website www.coa.uncc.edu

The College of Architecture has for over 12 years included a design-build program and offers a range of solar, sustainable, and integrated design courses, including sustainable planning studios.

Ohio

Cleveland Green Building Coalition

professional continuing education

Contact Melanie Kintner, *Director of Education*
3500 Lorain Avenue
Suite 200
Cleveland, OH 44113
216-961-8850
melanie@clevelandgbc.org
Website www.clevelandgbc.org
Periodical *Green Building News*

The purpose of the Cleveland Green Building Coalition is to advance green building in Cleveland and Northeast Ohio through education, consultation, and cooperation. The Cleveland GBC is an umbrella organization for various building industry interest groups, including those involved in residential, commercial, institutional, and industrial green building. The GBC works to coordinate green building efforts within Cleveland, and to aid and promote specific projects.

Ontario

Canada Green Building Council

professional

Contact Erica Mayer
330 - 55 rue Murray Street
Ottawa, ON K1N 5M3
613-241-1184
info@cagbc.org
Website www.cagbc.org

Similar to the USGBC, the relatively new Canada Green Building Council offers an intensive, one-day technical overview of the LEED Canada Green Building Rating System.

Everdale Environmental Learning Centre

continuing education hands-on

Contact Lynn Bishop, *Co-Founder*
PO Box 29
Hillsburgh, ON N0B 1Z0
519-855-4859
info@everdale.org
Website www.everdale.org

Everdale is a non-profit learning centre that teaches sustainable living by offering hands-on learning opportunities for people of all ages and backgrounds. The education programs are designed to make learning what it should be - an interactive and inspiring experience. Experts from the region provide instruction on topics ranging from solar and wind power to natural construction. The goal is to offer the kind of practical hands-on experience that can't be found in books or a classroom.

Kortright Centre

Contact Alex Waters
9550 Pine Valley Drive
Woodbridge, ON L4L 1A6
905-832-2289
kcc@look.ca
Website www.kortright.org

The Kortright Centre is one of Canada's largest environmental education facilities. Each year 130,000 students, families, and individuals attend our site and programs. Kortright is also a premise site for renewable energy and energy efficiency demonstrations and innovative programming.

The Pangea Partnership

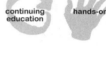

Contact Ron Stone, *Founder*
27 Beechwood Avenue
Suite 140
Ottawa, ON K1M 1M7
613-747-9185
rstone@pangeapartnership.org
Website www.pangeapartnership.org
Periodical *The Pangea Partnership*

The Pangea Partnership conducts workshops in developing nations that connect tourists with local youth. Participants learn how to construct healthy, ecological and economic buildings such as homes and schools. The workshops bring together international visitors with locals who will use what they learn in their communities. Participants are encouraged to take personal responsibility for global issues.

Sir Sandford Fleming College

Sustainable Building Design and Construction Program

Contact Ted Brandon, *Training Officer*
297 College Drive
Haliburton, ON K0M 1S0
705-457-1680
tbrandon@flemingc.on.ca
Website www.flemmingcollege.com

Fleming's new, leading-edge certificate program attracts students who wish to develop an integrated skill set in the design of structures using green, natural or sustainable building methods, technologies and materials, and renewable energy resources. Because the hands-on, practical component of this program involves construction of a sustainable building, the program is offered in an intensive compressed format for 20 weeks. The course workload is equivalent to a three-semester (45 week) program.

Aprovecho Research Center

continuing education
hands-on

Contact Jason Pruett
80574 Hazelton Road
Cottage Grove, OR 97424
541-942-8198
apro@efn.org
Website www.aprovecho.net
Periodical *News From Aprovecho*

Aprovecho Research Center conducts 10-week sustainable living skills internships. The three major areas of focus are sustainable forestry, appropriate technology, and organic gardening. Aprovecho has also experimented with alternative building design. Approximately 70-95 percent of the lumber used in the Center's buildings was sustainably harvested on-site.

Cob Cottage Company
North American School of Natural Building

continuing education
hands-on

Contact Jack Stephens, *Office Manager*
PO Box 123
Cottage Grove, OR 97424
541-942-2005
cobcottage@hotmail.com
Website www.cobcottage.com
Periodical *The Cob Web; The Hand Sculpted House*

North America's only comprehensive Natural Building School. Coastal temperate rainforest site, primitive facilities. The School teaches owner-builders, jumpstarts natural building professionals, does hands-on research, and publishes books and information on natural building. The Natural Building Colloquium, now in its 11th year, originated with the Cob Cottage Company. NASNB is an outgrowth of the Cob Cottage Company, started by Ianto Evans, Michael Smith, and Linda Smiley in 1993. The annual schedule lists 15-25 workshops including cob, bale-cob, natural plasters, earthen floors, living roofs, parent and child construction, and Pyromania!

Groundworks

continuing education
hands-on

Contact Becky Bee, *Founder*
PO Box 381
Murphy, OR 97533
541-471-3470
cobalot@cpros.com
Website www.cpros.com/~sequoia

Groundworks offers intensive, hands-on cob workshops and sponsors the Women's Natural Building Symposiums and Hands-On Extravaganzas. It has published two cob classics – *The Cob Builder's Handbook: You Can Hand Sculpt Your Own Home* and *You Can Make the Best Hot Tub Ever* – both by Becky Bee. The organization experiments, travels, hosts a show home, and networks with other natural building groups.

House Alive

Contact Coenraad Rogmans, *Founder*
7450 Griffin Lane
Jacksonville, OR 97530
541-889-3751
welcome@housealive.org
Website www.housealive.org

House Alive offers hands-on workshops in natural building with a focus on earthen construction and the use of locally available materials. Students gain the knowledge and confidence to begin an independent building project, whether it is a cob garden well or a natural home. The program covers everything from finding and preparing materials to finishing a structure with earthen plaster, as well as design techniques and appropriate technologies to improve the efficiency, health, and beauty of a home.

Portland Community College
Sustainable Building Certificate Program

Contact Mary Lou McCann
12000 S.W. 49th Avenue
Science Technology, Room 208
Portland, OR 97280
503-977-4163
mlmccann@pcc.edu
Website www.pcc.edu/pcc/pro/progs/arch/default.htm

The Sustainable Building Certificate program (currently pending state approval) provides course work from architecture, interior design, building construction, social sciences and science that relate to sustainable building issues. This program focuses on creating buildings that are sited, designed, constructed, operated, and maintained for the health and well being of the occupants, while minimizing impact on the environment. This program prepares designers and builders to develop buildings that protect occupant health; improve employee productivity; and are designed, built, renovated, operated, or reused in an ecological and resource-efficient manner.

University of Oregon

Contact Christine Theodoropulous, *Department Head*
322 Lawrence Hall
Suite 1206
Eugene, OR 97403-1206
541-346-3656
architecture@uoregon.edu
Website http://architecture.uoregon.edu

The University of Oregon Department of Architecture and other departments in the School of Architecture and Allied Arts (A&AA) have long strived to integrate sustainable design into fundamental design instruction. The School of A&AA is home to the Ecological Design Center, a student-run, faculty supported organization hosting ongoing programs and an annual conference in ecological design. The Department of Architecture provides a comprehensive and holistic approach to learning - stressing issues of program, site and building technology, by teaching the skills for developing informed and meaningful intentions and the capability to translate intentions into highly resolved and sustainable design. In keeping with its building science tradition, the University of Oregon is also home to the Agents of Change Program.

Pennsylvania

Carnegie Mellon University

Contact Stephen R. Lee, *Professor*
5000 Forbes Avenue
Pittsburgh, PA 15213-3890
412-268-2350
stevelee@cmu.edu
Website www.arc.cmu.edu/cmu/index.jsp

Sustainability is a primary focus of the Carnegie Mellon School of Architecture, which now offers a Master of Science degree in Sustainable Design. The University's Center for Building Performance and Diagnostics conducts research, development, and demonstrations in advanced building technologies and systems integration for high performance buildings, in improved approaches to the building delivery process, and in workplace productivity. The faculty of the CBPD possesses an interdisciplinary and complementary combination of backgrounds. Its expertise includes professional practice, fundamental and applied research in building sciences, advanced computer modeling and simulation, and post occupancy evaluation.

Rhode Island

Apeiron Institute

Contact Bradley Grove Hyson, *Executive Director*
451 Hammet Road
Coventry, RI 02816
401-397-3430
info@apeiron.org
Website www.apeiron.org

The Apeiron Institute is a nonprofit organization bringing sustainable living practices from around the world to Southern New England through education and advocacy. The Institute helps people understand the connection between their lifestyle and the environment, offering solutions to improve well-being while reducing environmental impact. The year-round adult program calendar includes workshops, study circles, speakers, and special events on issues including renewable energy, ecological building, deep ecology, and sustainable living. Apeiron is also the driving force behind the Rhode Island Sustainability Coalition.

Tennessee

Eco-Village Training Center

Contact Albert Bates, *Founder*
189 Schoolhouse Road
Summertown, TN 38483
931-964-4324
ecovillage@thefarm.org
Website www.thefarm.org/etc

The Ecovillage Training Center is part of the Global Village Institute for Appropriate Technology, which has been pushing the frontiers of alternative energy, housing, farming, and tools for sustainability for the past 20 years. The Ecovillage Training Center consists of a whole systems immersion experience of ecovillage living, together with classes of instruction, access to information, tools and resources, and on-site and off-site consulting and outreach experiences.

Texas

Center for Maximum Potential Building Systems

continuing education

Contact Gail Vittori, *Co-Director*
8604 FM 969
Austin, TX 78724
512-928-4786
center@cmpbs.org
Website www.cmpbs.org

CMPBS uses life-cycle design to foster ecological balance within a multi-scalar context and engages in interdisciplinary collaborations with a common vision of healthful environments, economic prosperity, and social equity. Since 1990, the Center has offered a limited number of credit- and non-credit based internships. The interdisciplinary approach bridges hands-on, practical work experiences with CMPBS projects that draw on the intern's skills and interests.

....

University of Texas at Austin

higher education

Contact Dr. Steven A. Moore, *Program Director*
1 University Station
Suite B7500
Austin, TX 78712
512-471-0184
samoore@mail.utexas.edu
Website http://web.austin.utexas.edu/architecture/academic/main.html

The Graduate Sustainable Design Program at the University of Texas is housed in the School of Architecture and offers four degree programs: The First Professional (MArch 1) program for students without a professional degree in architecture, the Post-Professional (MArch 2) program for students with a professional degree in architecture, the MSSD (Master of Science in Sustainable Design) for graduate students who wish to pursue research or teaching as a career, and the PhD in History as an Interdisciplinary program.

Virginia

Green Advantage

professional

Contact Grady O'Rear
12606 Trillium Glen Lane
Taylorstown, VA 20180
540-822-9449
gorear@greenadvantage.org
Website www.greenadvantage.org

Green Advantage is an environmental certification for building-related practitioners – particularly contractors, sub-contractors, and trades people. Certified individuals have demonstrated knowledge of green building principles, materials, and techniques in order to pass the Green Advantage Certification Exam. Launched with the US Environmental Protection Agency and Nature Conservancy monies, Green Advantage is an Educational Partner of the US Green Building Council.

University of Virginia

higher education

Contact Bruce Dotson, *Associate Professor*
Campbell Hall
PO Box 400122
Charlottesville, VA 22904
434-924-7019
dotson@virginia.edu
Website www.virginia.edu/arch/

The School of Architecture at the University of Virginia supports a design ethic that critically engages three areas of design research: the interdependence of cultural forces and ecological processes; the ethical choices inherent in construction; and the implications of emerging technology for design. The SoA values environments where rural character is protected, where cities have vital centers, and where neighbors offer housing for all. Historic preservation and public history are important concerns as we plan for the future.

Vermont

Yestermorrow Design/Build School

professional continuing education hands-on

Contact Patricia Pinkston, *Executive Director*
189 VT Route 100
Warren, VT 05674
802-496-5545
designbuild@yestermorrow.org
Website www.yestermorrow.org
Periodical Course Catalog

Since 1980, Yestermorrow has been the only design/build school in the country, teaching both design and construction skills. Specializing in residential design, ecologically-sound construction, and fine woodworking, our 2-day to 2-week hands-on courses are taught by top architects, builders, and craftspeople from across the country. For people of all ages and experience, novice to professional.

Washington

Lighting Design Lab

professional

Contact Diana Grant, *Project Manager*
400 E. Pine Street
Suite 100
Seattle, WA 98122
800-354-3864
diana.grant@seattle.gov
Website www.lightingdesignlab.com/index.html
Periodical *Lighting Design Lab NEWS*

The Lighting Design Lab wants to transform the Northwest lighting market by promoting quality design and energy efficient technologies. The Lab has operated throughout the Pacific Northwest since 1989. The Lab accomplishes its mission through education and training, consultations, technical assistance, and demonstrations. The Lab serves Idaho, Montana, Oregon, and Washington.

Seattle Central Community College
Sustainable Building Advisor Certificate Program

professional

Contact Katherine Morgan
Seattle Central Community College
1701 Broadway 2 BE4180J
Seattle, WA 98122
206-842-8995
Website www.sustainableseattle.net/

The Sustainable Building Advisor Certificate Program is a learning experience designed for working professionals. Nine-month specialized training program enables graduates to advise employers or clients on strategies and tools for implementing sustainable building. Utilizes expert instructors, interactive format, team project analyses, and opportunity for national certification through an exam.

....

Western Washington University

higher education

Contact Arunas Oslapas, *Professor*
Department of Engineering Technology
MS 9086
Bellingham, WA
360-650-3425
arunas.oslapas@wwu.edu
Website www.ac.wwu.edu/~huxley/

Western Washington University's Huxley College of the Environment and the Engineering Technology Department jointly offer a minor in Sustainable Design. The minor provides basic foundations in environmental studies and design, and allows for individualized tailoring according to the student's interests.

Wisconsin

Energy Center of Wisconsin

continuing education

Contact Marge Anderson, *Education & Outreach*
Madison, WI
608-238-4601
ecw@ecw.org
Website www.ecw.org

The Energy Center of Wisconsin has the capabilities to train audiences from any sector on any energy-efficiency related subject. In the past five years, ECW has provided more than 360 training programs for nearly 14,600 participants – and twice won the Award for Excellence in Education from the American Institute of Architects' Continuing Education System. Recent activities include a Building Operator Certification Program, a Cool Daylighting™ Training Series, a Smarter Buildings: Smarter Business Conference, an Industries of the Future Symposium and a Technical Trainer's Toolbox.

University of Wisconsin at Milwaukee

Contact Jim Wasley, *Associate Professor*
School of Architecture and Urban Planning
PO Box 413
Milwaukee, WI 53201-0413
414-229-4014
jwasley@uwm.edu
Website www.uwm.edu/SARUP/index.html

higher education

The study of architecture at the University of Wisconsin at Milwaukee is a six-year program consisting of three levels and leading to the accredited professional degree of Master of Architecture. UWM places a strong emphasis on building science, including solar energy and efficient standards, and Professor Jim Wasley is current President of the Society of Building Science Educators (SBSE).

Additional Resources

4

- Curriculum Resources
- Related Organizations
- Individual Instructors

Curriculum Resources

Agents of Change

Contact Allison Kwok, *Associate Professor*
Agents of Change Lab
Department of Architecture
1206 University of Oregon
Eugene, OR 97403
541-346-2126
akwok@uoregon.edu
Website http://aoc.uoregon.edu/

Agents of Change is a building-science-oriented program funded by the U.S. Department of Education Fund for the Improvement of Postsecondary Education (FIPSE), initially in 2000 then from 2002-2005. Through Agents of Change, faculty and teaching assistants from accredited architecture programs have been trained to investigate actual buildings, conduct post-occupancy surveys, and develop exercises to implement at their home institutions. University of Oregon Graduate Teaching Fellows and Society of Building Science Educators (SBSE, see listing below) faculty with extensive experience in the procedures lead teams through exercises, protocols, and the case study approach drawn from the Vital Signs Project (see listing below).

Agents of Change provides written, customizable "building investigation" exercises with loaner equipment sets for participants in the Agents of Change training sessions who will use them to implement case study exercises in their classes. Program resources are made available on the Agents of Change website, where they will continue to reside following the close of this round of funded activity.

....

Curriculum Information Database

Society of Building Science Educators (SBSE)

Contact Jim Wasley, *President*
Department of Architecture
c/o University of Wisconsin - Milwaukee
PO Box 413
Milwaukee, WI 53201
jwasley@uwm.edu
Website www.sbse.org/

SBSE is in the process of developing an on-line database of curriculum offerings related to building science, including descriptions of required building science courses at North American architecture schools and a sampling of descriptions of building science electives. When made available during the Summer of 2005, the database will include: building science course descriptions, course length and credit hours, the year-level(s) the course is geared toward, and links to copies of course materials.

Ecological Literacy in Architectural Education

Contact Erika Taylor
The American Institute of Architects,
Committee on the Environment (COTE)
1735 New York Avenue, NW
Washington, DC 20006
800-AIA-3837
etaylor@aia.org
Website www.aia.org/COTE/

Under a Tides Foundation grant, COTE has undertaken an initiative to encourage the development of ecological design instructional tools. In a competition closing in February 2005, schools of architecture were asked to submit descriptions, for coursework and programs related to sustainability and ecological literacy for monetary awards of $3,000 to schools, one in each in the following broad categories:

1. Environmental Foundations in Architecture
2. Integrated Systems Design
3. Sustainable Community Design

Submissions in the above categories are to be reviewed by a panel of COTE representatives and the data will be incorporated into an outline of potential education strategies, and a compilation of selected submissions will be included as part of a report for general distribution later in 2005.

Educating Architects for a Sustainable Environment (EASE)

Contact Marvin Rosenman, AIA & Joseph Bilello, Ph.D., AIA
College of Architecture and Planning
AB 104
Ball State University
Muncie, IN 47306
765-285-5859
Website http://jbilello.iweb.bsu.edu/ease/

The EASE Project conferences in 1994 and 1995 led to the development of a series of EASE Recommendations for sustainable design education, specific implementation strategies for the EASE Recommendations and the proposal of several model curricula to be built around these strategies. From a myriad of new potential curriculum models and variations on existing models, five models were chosen for development by EASE participants, for which detailed descriptions are available on the EASE Project website:

1. Health, Safety, Welfare Redefinition Curriculum
2. Design and Build Curriculum
3. Split Program Curriculum
4. Whole-systems Curriculum
5. Knowledge-based Curriculum

Green Architecture Curriculum Project

Contact Ecotone LLC
PO Box 7147
Kansas City, MO 64113
816-363-3304
info@ecotonedesign.com
Website www.ecotonedesign.com

Ecotone, a new publishing company dedicated to sustainable design, has launched an interactive curriculum development project in partnership with participating design schools. Ecotone will begin with the creation of a draft study guide based on Jason McLennan's The Philosophy of Sustainable Design while participating professors use the book in at least one class for a minimum of one semester. Over the course of the project, the draft study guide will be updated and expanded based input from the faculty and students using the guide, following which Ecotone plans to publish a small 'handbook' that contains the expanded study guide along with the best samples from student work and instructor teaching ideas, which will ultimately lead to the first edition of a textbook.

....

Green Design Education Initiative

Website www.idec.org/greendesign/home.html

The Green Design Education Initiative is a partnership of the Interior Design Educators Council (IDEC), the International Interior Design Association (IIDA), the International Facility Management Association (IFMA) and Metropolis Magazine. The magazine and these associations collaborated in the development of Interior Design course modules in the following subjects, available on their website:

1. Ecology and the Built Environment
2. Environmental Attitudes and Sustainability
3. Environmental Technologies for Interiors
4. Interior Materials
5. Introduction to Sustainable Interior Design Methodology
6. MEPS: Material Performance Evaluation System

....

Greening the Curricula / Verdir le Diplôme

Contact Ray Cole, University of British Colombia
Organization of book publication
raycole@arch.ubc.ca
Contact Daniel Pearl, Université de Montréal
Organization of book publication
daniel.pearl@umontreal.ca
Contact Richard Kroeker, Dalhousie University
Organization of traveling exhibition
richard.kroeker@dal.ca
Contact André Potvin, Université Laval
Organization of symposium details and website
andre.potvin@arc.ulaval.ca
Website www.greening-verdir.arc.ulaval.ca/index.html

Phase 1 of Greening the Curricula / Verdir le Diplôme took place in 2002, with Phase 2 following in 2004. The website contains symposia documentation as well as information on follow-up activites.

LEED® Reference Guide, Training Workbook and Speaker Notes

Contact U.S. Green Building Council
1015 18th Street, NW
Suite 508
Washington, DC 20036
202-82-USGBC
workshop@usgbc.org
Website www.usgbc.org

The LEED Reference Guide is a publicly available manual including explanations of LEED Green Building Rating System prerequisite and credit requirements, as well as background information, suggested technologies and strategies, explanations of referenced standards, and selected case studies. The LEED Training Workbook and Speaker Notes are made available to LEED Workshop participants as part of the workshop fee. Both sets of information serve as useful preparation materials for the LEED Professional Accreditation Exam.

....

NCARB Monographs

Contact National Council of Architectural Registration Boards (NCARB)
1801 K Street, NW
Suite 1100-K
Washington, DC 20006
202-783-6500
customerservice@ncarb.org
Website www.ncarb.org/publications/pdpmonographs.html

NCARB has created a series of monographs intended as preparation for self-study on-line quizzes earning leaning units in Health Welfare and Safety. Titles related to ecological design and building include:

- Sustainable Design (147 pages)
- Energy-Conscious Architecture (76 pages)
- Getting to Smart Growth (97 pages)

....

RedVector.com

Contact Two Urban Centre
4890 W. Kennedy Boulevard
Suite 740
Tampa, FL 33609
866-546-1212
clientsupport@RedVector.com
Website www.redvector.com

RedVector.com provides online courses and reference materials in "Sustainable / Green Design", among other technical subject categories for engineers, designers, and builders. All courses presented are pre-approved for credit with those state boards and professional organizations that require pre-approval.

Report Card on Ecological Design Education

Contact Northwest Alliance for Ecological Design Education
Heather Flint
alliancenw@yahoo.com

The NW Alliance for Ecological Design Education (a coalition of student, faculty & professionals) is proposing a multi-campus assessment of universities and colleges throughout the Pacific Northwest. This systematic assessment will evaluate design and planning schools based on their availability of faculty, courses, degree programs, advisors, and research in ecological design. The final output will be a "Report Card" highlighting successes, areas for improvement and overall leadership in eco-design education, including case studies of key programs/ projects/ research, and summary tables providing a comparative ranking of institutions demonstrating excellence in eco-design education. The NW Alliance and its partners will conduct the research during 2005 and publish and distribute the Report Card to major universities nationally in April 2006. Follow-up activities will include securing funding to sponsor annual report card production (research, publication and distribution), as well as related activities to help foster increased communication among design schools throughout the Pacific Northwest.

....

Sustainable Environmental Design Education (SEDE) *

Contact Margot McDonald, *Professor*
Architecture Department and Renewable Energy Institute
California Polytechnic State University
San Luis Obispo, CA 93407
805-756-1298
sede@calpoly.edu
Website www.calpoly.edu/~sede/home.html

The California Integrated Waste Management Board (CIWMB) together with the Renewable Energy Institute at Cal Poly-San Luis Obispo (REI) undertook a project from March 2002 to May 2004 to improve the adoption of sustainable environmental design principles in higher education and industry continuing education programs in architecture and landscape architecture. The website presents the curriculum model, including numerous sample course syllabi, including those from currently offered courses as well as proposed courses. Also included are descriptions teaching methods, results of two extensive surveys on environmental design education, and abundant additional resources. The website is intended to both present the results of the study and to serve as a dissemination tool to share the materials developed with educators.

....

Sustainable Facilities and Infrastructure Program

Contact Georgia Tech Research Institute
SHETD/EOEML
Atlanta, GA 30332
404-894-7429
Website http://maven.gtri.gatech.edu/sfi/gradcourses/courses.html

Georgia Tech's currently dormant Sustainable Facilities & Infrastructure Program took the noteworthy step of making their previously offered graduate and undergraduate course syllabi and resource materials publicly available on-line.

Vital Signs

Contact Charles C. Benton (Cris)
College of Environmental Design
390 Wurster Hall
University of California, Berkeley
Berkeley, CA 9472
510-642-0669
crisp@socrates.berkeley.edu
Website www.arch.ced.berkeley.edu/vitalsigns/Default.htm

The Vital Signs Project, funded through 1998, emphasized building awareness about the numerous ways in which their design decisions affect a building's physical performance--from energy use, to indoor environmental quality, to occupant well-being. As part of the Vital Signs Project, twelve faculty members from architecture schools in the United States and Canada developed a series of flexible, modular "Resource Packages" that address physical building performance issues such as energy use, the experiential qualities of buildings, and occupant well being. Each package provides protocols for the field evaluation of existing buildings, activities that have been used to create written "Building Case Studies" describing student findings. Resource packages, case studies and other materials are currently available on the project's website.

* Charts on the following two pages:

Scope of Curriculum from Sustainable Environmental Design Education (SEDE)

To provide instructors of architecture and landscape architecture related design programs with a comprehensive overview of the content (columns a-d), skills (column e), and requisite knowledge (column f) for sustainable design, SEDE derived a matrix consisting of the ten fundamental concerns that should be addressed in an ideal curriculum model. The topics are not arranged in a particular curricular sequence.
[Reproduced courtesy of SEDE].

	A. Definitions	B. Human and Natural Systems Relationships	C. Scales of Influence
1. Design & Natural Systems	*Planetary systems and dynamics*: bio-geo-chemical; climatological; ecological; hydrological	*Ethical issues and theories*: environmentalism; permaculture; regenerative design	*Patterns and scale in nature*: biomes; bioregion; watersheds; bio-communities; landscapes
2. Design & Agricultural Systems	*Human systems and dynamics*: anthropology; cultural geography; human ecology; history	*Socio-cultural issues and the built environment*: accessibility; demographics; human factors; growth impacts; planning; social justice	*Patterns and scale in human communities*: urban; rural; suburban
3. Design & Economic Systems	*Economic systems and resource flows*: human, natural, and economic capital	*Ecology, ethics and economic theory*: natural step; triple bottom line	*Economies of scale*: global; regional; local; small is beautiful; limits to growth
4. Design & Information Systems	*Communication and information systems*: verbal; graphical; written; symbolic and pictorial	*Information and social impacts on the built environment*: participatory design; telecommuting	*Communication networks*: global; regional; local; Internet/Intranet
5. Desgin & Aesthetic Systems	*Human perception of sensory (visual, auditory, thermal, etc.) deslight in the environment*: sense of place	*Social issues relating aesthetic experience*: age; cultural; income; gender; politics; values	*Forms of human aesthetic experience in the environment*: acoustical; aqueous; haptic; kinesthetic; thermal; visual; spatial
6. Design & Structural Systems	*Structural system integration*, economic, environmental, social, & aesthetic factors of structure	*Social and ethical issues of structural systems*: embodied energy; environmental factors; demountability; labor force; structural effieciency	*Scale of structural system components*: roofs; walls; floors; foundations; columns & beams; paving systems
7. Design & Material Resources	*Materials of the built environment*: economic, environment, social, & aesthetic issues of building and landscape materials	*Social and ethical issues of materials*: human health; environmental impacts; labor issues; local resources	*Material properties*: acoustical; dimensional; thermal; "greenness"; cost
8. Design & Energy Resources	*Bioclimatic design in the built environment*: solar, wind, biomass and hydro resources as economic, enviro., social & aesthetic solutions	*Philosophy of energy issues*: "soft path"; centralized; independent; environmental impacts	*Building and land metabolism*: scale; comfort; appropriate technology; whole systems
9. Design & Bio-Resources	*Regeneration in agriculture, landscapes, water & built enviros.*: water cycle; nutrient cycle; land-air-water exchanges	*Philosophies of resource conservation*: land ethic; waste=food; habitat restoration; resource recover; soil regeneration	*Land coverage by scale*: regional; landscapes; large scale farms; urban agriculture

	D. History and Evolution	E. Techniques	F. Prerequisites
1. Design & Natural Systems	*Natural history*: climate; micro-climate; flora & fauna; resources	*Techniques*: site analysis; planning & design; landscape ecology; GIS/GPS	*Prequisites*: biology; botany; chemistry; ecology; mathematics
2. Design & Agricultural Systems	*Cultural history and change in built enviro.*: cultural identity; pre-historic & historic bldgs; landscapes; settlement patterns	*Techniques*: activity analysis; archival research; personal interviews; programming	*Prerequisites*: history; planning; social sciences; statistics
3. Design & Economic Systems	*Evolution of environmental economics*: ecology of commerce	*Techniques*: life-cycle analysis; ecological footprint	*Prerequisites*: accounting; economics; mathematics
4. Design & Information Systems	*Evolution of information systems & technology*: computing; GIS/GPS; CAD/CAM	*Techniques*: freehand; CAD/CAM; GPS/GIS; virtual reality; smart objects	*Prerequisites*: computing; drawing; graphic design; mathematics; speech; technical writing
5. Desgin & Aesthetic Systems	*Evolution of aesthetic systems*: avant-garde; baroque; classical; organic; post-modern, etc.	*Techniques*: architecture; dance/drama; drawing; enviro. art; furniture/graphic/industrial/ interior/landscape design; painting/sculpture; textiles	*Prerequisites*: basic design; drawing; history (e.g., art); model-making
6. Design & Structural Systems	*Evolution of structural systems*: indigenous, man-made; hi-tech; high performance materials	*Techniques*: post-and-beam; masonry/ concrete; tensile; thin shell concrete	*Prerequisites*: chemistry; mathematics; statistics; strength of materials; physics
7. Design & Material Resources	*Evolution of materials*: vernacular; man-made; high performance; industrial ecology; biomimicy	*Techniques*: recycled/recyclable; compostable; alternatives (materials and methods); healthy materials	*Prerequisites*: business; chemistry; construction; physics; structures
8. Design & Energy Resources	*Evolution of energy sources & systems*: solar, wind, biomass hydro, and non-renewable resources	*Techniques*: passive solar; heating & cooling; low energy systems; efficient HVAC; anaerobic digestion; daylighting; bldg. commissioning	*Prequisites*: design with climate; earth science; ecology; engineering; mathematics; physics
9. Design & Bio-Resources	*History & evolution of natural resources:* forests; farmland; water	*Techniques*: anaerobic digestion; constructed wetlands; holistic resource mgt.; permaculture; graywater; rainwater catchment	*Prerequisites*: agriculture; biology; chemistry; ecology; engineering; enviro.; planning; landscape ecology; resource mgt.

Related Organizations

This section includes organizations that focus on ecological design and building issues and that offer periodic educational and advocacy programs. Also included are organizations focused on environmental education and career preparation, inclusive of, but not limited to, ecological design and building.

Arizona

Arizona Solar Center

Dan Aiello, *Chairman*
c/o Janus II - Environmental Architects
4309 E. Marion Way
Phoenix, AZ 85018
602-952-8192
solar@azsolarcenter.com
www.azsolarcenter.com

Not-for-profit resource center dedicated to promoting the use and technological awareness of solar and renewable energy in Arizona and the Southwestern US.

....

Development Center for Appropriate Technology (DCAT)

David Eisenberg, *Executive Director*
PO Box 27513
Tucson, AZ 85726
520-624-6628
info@dcat.net
www.dcat.net

Organization dedicated to creating a sustainable context for business codes and standards. Also offers consultation services on alternative construction systems, such as strawbale.

....

Scottsdale Green Building Program

Anthony Floyd, *Sustainable Building Manager*
7447 E. Indian School Road
Suite 125
Scottsdale, AZ 85251
480-312-4202
www.scottsdaleaz.gov/greenbuilding

Local program advocating a whole-systems approach to design and construction to reduce environmental impact and energy consumption.

British Columbia

Greater Vancouver Regional District's BuildSmart

Helen Goodland, *Senior Business Advisor*
Greater Vancouver Regional District Head Office
4330 Kingsway
Burnaby, BC V5H 4G8
604-451-6575
buildsmart@gvrd.bc.ca
www.gvrd.bc.ca/buildsmart/

Program of the Greater Vancouver Regional District encouraging the use of green building strategies and technologies; supporting green building efforts by offering tools and technical resources; and educating the building industry on sustainable design and building practices.

....

Green Buildings BC

Program Coordinator
Vancouver, BC
www.greenbuildingsbc.com

Regional initiative promoting efficient building practices for health care and educational facilities.

....

California

Architects / Designers / Planners for Social Responsibility (ADPSR)

Raphael Sperry, *National President*
PO Box 9126
Berkeley, CA 94709-0126
510-845-1000
forum@adpsr.org
www.adpsr.org

National organization with local chapters dedicated to promoting social and environmental justice through responsible design and planning.

ArchVoices
Editor
1014 Curtis Street
Albany, CA 94706
510-757-6213
editors@archvoices.org
www.archvoices.org
ArchVoices Newsletter

An independent, not-for-profit organization focused on architectural education, internship and licensure.

....

Build it Green
Program Manager
PO Box 11944
Berkeley, CA 94712
info@builditgreen.org
www.builditgreen.org

Regional not-for-profit group providing information about healthy, durable, energy and resource-efficient residential and commercial building to the general public, building professionals and local governments.

....

California Straw Building Association
Joy Bennett, *Co-Director*
PO Box 1293
Angels Camp, CA 95222
209-785-7077
casba@strawbuilding.org
www.strawbuilding.org
CASBA Newsletter

Membership organization focused on the development of strawbale construction technique through the exchange of practical knowledge, research and testing.

....

Ecological Design Institute
Sim Van der Ryn, *Founder*
PO Box 989
Sausalito, CA 94966
415-332-5806
va@ecodesign.org
www.ecodesign.org

Currently inactive organization founded to explore and improve the relationships between nature, culture, and technology. Creator of the EDEN Program.

Global Green USA
Matt Peterson, *President and CEO*
2218 Main Street
2nd Floor
Santa Monica, CA 90405
310-581-2700
ggusa@globalgreen.org
www.globalgreen.org
Solar City Report; A Blueprint for Greening Affordable Housing

United States affiliate of Green Cross International facilitating reduced environmental impact and equitable resources through education and advocacy.

....

Urban Ecology
Diana M. Williams, *Executive Director*
414 13th Street
Suite 500
Oakland, CA 94612
510-251-6330
urbanecology@urbanecology.org
www.urbanecology.org

Multi-disciplinary organization focused on developing healthy, ecological urban environments through responsible design, planning and alternative transportation.

....

Colorado

American Solar Energy Society
Program Director
2400 Central Avenue
Suite A
Boulder, CO 80301
303-443-3130
ases@ases.org
www.ases.org
SOLAR TODAY; Advances in Solar Energy

Professional organization dedicated to advancing the development and use of solar and other renewable energy technologies in buildings and industry. National organization with 23 state and regional chapters.

Colorado Straw Bale Association (COSBA)
Mark Schueneman, *Executive* Director
2010 Hermosa Drive
Boulder, CO 80304
303-444-6027
costrawbale@yahoo.com
www.coloradostrawbale.org
The COSBA Update

Membership organization focused on the development of strawbale construction technique through shared knowledge and experience.

....

Green Points Program
Elizabeth Vasatka, *Environmental Coordinator*
City of Boulder
Green Points Program
PO Box 791
Boulder, CO 80306
303-441-1964
vasatkae@ci.boulder.co.us
www.ci.boulder.co.us/environmentalaffairs

Local government program developed to encourage sustainable design and renovation methods that conserve natural resources.

....

Institute for Sustainable Power
Board Member
PO Box 2558
Evergreen, CO 80437
303-679-3068
roger_w_taylor@hotmail.com
www.ispq.org

International not-for-profit organization focused on the improvement of renewable energy projects and the development of sustainable, local jobs within the renewable energy sector.

Rocky Mountain Institute
Amory B. Lovins, *CEO*
1739 Snowmass Creek Road
Snowmass, CO 81654
970-927-3851
outreach@rmi.org
www.rmi.org
RMI Solutions; Natural Capitalism

Entrepreneurial not-for-profit organization fostering efficient use of resources through innovative solutions in business, culture and government.

....

District of Columbia

American Council for an Energy-Efficient Economy
Steven Nadel, *Executive Director*
1001 Connecticut Avenue NW
Suite 801
Washington, DC 20036
202-429-8873
info@aceee.org
www.aceee.org
ACEEE's Grapevine

Not-for-profit organization focused on the advancement of energy efficiency to benefit both the environment and the economy.

....

American Institute of Architects - Committee on the Environment (AIA COTE)
Erika Taylor, *Project Manager*
1735 New York Avenue NW
Washington, DC 20006
202-626-7407
cote@aia.org
www.aia.org/cote

Knowledge community of the American Institute of Architects focused on advancing the knowledge and application of environmentally responsible design practices In the U.S. AIA COTE sponsors conferences, competitions and other outreach and advocacy activities geared toward architects and related professionals. National Committee with 43 state and local chapter committees.

Association of Collegiate Schools of Architecture (ACSA) - Task Force on Sustainability

Kim Tanzer, *Chair*
1735 New York Avenue NW, 3rd Floor
Washington, DC 20005
202-785-2324
info@acsa-arch.org
www.acsa-arch.org

ACSA's Task Force on Sustainability met in 2003 and made a series of recommendations to the Architectural Accrediting Board (NAAB) in a memo regarding "strengthening NAAB criteria to reflect a commitment to the principles of sustainability within architectural curricula."

....

Association of University Leaders for a Sustainable Future (ULSF)

Wynn Calder, *Associate Director*
2100 L Street NW
Washington, DC 20037
202-778-6133
info@ulsf.org
www.ulsf.org
The Declaration; US Progress Toward Sustainability in Higher Education

Organization dedicated to assisting international institutions of higher education in holistically integrating principles of sustainability. Acts as the secretariat for signatories of the Talloires Declaration, a commitment to environmental sustainability.

....

Energy Star Program

Program Director
US EPA Climate Protection Partnership Division (MS-6202J)
1200 Pennsylvania Avenue NW
Washington, DC 20460
888-782-7937
www.energystar.gov

U.S. government program providing standards, tools and trainings for achieving maximum energy efficiency in buildings and consumer products.

GreenHOME, Inc.

Patty Rose, *Executive Director*
PO Box 42676
Washington, DC 20016
202-544-5336
pattyrose@greenhome.org
www.greenhome.org
Green and Learn

Regional group working to make affordable, sustainable residential design and construction commonplace practice through programs in education, technical assistance, construction and demonstration, and policy.

....

Healthy Building Network

Bill Walsh, *Founder and National Coordinator*
927 15th Street NW, 4th Floor
Washington, DC 20005
202-898-1610
info@healthybuilding.net
www.healthybuilding.net
Healthy Building News

National network of green professionals and socially responsible advocates interested in improving health and environmental impact through healthier building materials. A program of the Institute for Local Self Reliance.

....

National Institute of Building Sciences

David A. Harris, *President*
1090 Vermont Avenue NW
Suite 700
Washington, DC 20005
202-289-7800
nibs@nibs.org
www.nibs.org
Building Sciences Newsletter

Not-for-profit non-governmental organization that conducts studies, carries out projects, and facilitates discussion between government representatives and building science professionals to improve safe, affordable construction.

Partnership for Advancing Technology in Housing (PATH)
Program Director
451 7th Street SW
Suite 8134
Washington, DC 20410
800-245-2691
pathnet@pathnet.org
www.pathnet.org
PATH Quarterly

Public-private partnership accelerating the implementation of emerging of technologies that improve the life, energy-efficiency, environmental performance and affordability of housing. Administered by the US Department of Housing and Urban Development (HUD).

....

Sustainable Buildings Industry Council
Helen English, *Executive Director*
1112 16th Street NW
Suite 240
Washington, DC 20036
202-628-7400
sbic@sbicouncil.org
www.sbicouncil.org
Buildings Inside and Out

Professional organization providing guidelines, software, tools and trainings focused on sustainable design and energy analyses. Formerly the Passive Solar Industries Council.

....

US Green Building Council - Education Committee
Tom Rogers, *Committee Chair*
1015 18th Street NW
Suite 508
Washington, DC 20036
202-828-7422
education@committees.usgbc.org
www.usgbc.org

USGBC organizational committee dedicated to recommending action items to the Board of Directors in support of educational programs, college curriculum development, certification programs and outreach.

Florida

Florida Green Building Coalition
Program Director
3511 Santiago Way
Naples, FL 34105
239-263-6819
info@floridagreenbuilding.org
www.floridagreenbuilding.org

State-wide not-for-profit organization dedicated to improving the built environment through green building practices.

....

Georgia

ASHRAE Learning Institute
T. Fisher
1791 Tullie Circle, N.E.
Atlanta, GA 30329
800- 527-4723
tfisher@ashrae.org
www.ashrae.org

Provides online and on-site training opportunities in conjunction with ASHRAE events and activities.

....

Association of Energy Engineers (AEE)
Executive Director
4025 Pleasantdale Road
Suite 420
Atlanta, GA 30340
770-447-5083
info@aeecenter.org
www.aeecenter.org
Energy Engineering; Energy Insight

Membership organization focused on energy efficiency, utility deregulation and environmental compliance.

Maryland

Green Building Institute at the EnviroCenter
Jack Arnold, *Director*
152 Blades Lane
Unit N
Glen Burnie, MD 21060
410-768-4041
info@enviro-center.org
www.enviro-center.org

Not-for-profit educational program located at the EnviroCenter founded to encourage sustainable building practices through example, education and research. Educational activities to begin after construction of EnviroCenter green office building is completed.

....

National Association of Home Builders (NAHB) Research Center
Richard Dooley, *Environmental Analyst/Land Use Planner*
400 Prince George's Boulevard
Upper Marlboro, MD 20774
301-430-6242
www.nahbrc.org
Green Building Guidelines

Subsidiary of the National Association of Home Builders dedicated to advancing technology and affordability by facilitating liaisons between residential professionals, government and housing industries.

....

Massachusetts

The Green Roundtable, Inc.
Barbra Batshalom, *Executive Director*
7 Winthrop Square
Boston, MA 02110
info@greenroundtable.org
www.greenroundtable.org

Independent non-profit organization and affiliate of the USGBC whose mission is to mainstream sustainable development, and provide education, policy and technical assistance to local governments, building owners and institutions.

Northeast Sustainable Energy Association (NESEA)
Nancy Hazard, *Executive Director*
50 Miles Street
Greenfield, MA 01301
413-774-6051
nesea@nesea.org
www.nesea.org
Northeast Sun

Regional not-for-profit education and advocacy organization accelerating the deployment of renewable energy, energy efficiency and green buildings through conferences, referral service, K-12 curricula, and public events.

....

Ocean Arks International
Dr. John Todd, *President*
10 Shanks Pond Road
Falmouth, MA 02540
508-548-8161
jtodd@cape.com
www.oceanarks.org
Annals of Earth

Center dedicated to adapting ecological design science and practice for world-wide communities.

....

Second Nature
Anthony Cortese, *President*
PO Box 120007, Boston, MA 02112
617-576-1395
acortese@secondnature.org
www.secondnature.org

Organization focused on integrating sustainability into higher education.

....

Michigan

Center for Sustainable Systems
Helaine R. Hunscher, *Program Coordinator*
440 Church Street, Dana Building
Ann Arbor, MI 48109-1041
734-764-1412
css.info@umich.edu
http://css.snre.umich.edu

A research, education, and outreach center housed within the University of Michigan, advancing sustainability by developing and applying life cycle models and sustainability metrics for systems that meet societal needs.

Montana

National Center for Appropriate Technology (NCAT)

Kathy Hadley, *Executive Director*
PO Box 3838
Butte, MT 59702
800-275-6228
info@ncat.org
www.ncat.org
Weekly Harvest; ATTRAnews

National organization dedicated to improving economically disadvantaged communities by providing access to appropriate technology use and information.

....

Sage Mountain Center

Christopher Borton, *Director*
79 Sage Mountain Trail
Whitehall, MT 59759
406-494-9875
smc@sagemountain.org
www.sagemountain.org

Center focused on fostering inner growth, physical health, and sustainable living that integrate personal and global awareness.

....

Nebraska

Green Prairie Foundation for Sustainability

Joyce Coppinger, *Coordinator*
PO Box 22706
Lincoln, NE 68542-2706
402-483-5135
thelaststraw@thelaststraw.org
www.thelaststraw.org/GPFS/index.html
The Last Straw Jounal

Organization supporting and developing the use of sustainable building materials and other renewable resources through cooperative ventures. The Foundation publishes *The Last Straw Journal*, a quarterly journal focused on strawbale and natural building materials. Also hosts the Straw Bale Association of Nebraska (SBAN) and the Mid-America Straw Bale Association (MASBA).

Lincoln Green Building Group

Joyce Coppinger, *Coordinator*
PO Box 22706
Lincoln, NE 68542-2706
402-483-5135
info@lincolngreenbuildinggroup.com
www.lincolngreenbuildinggroup.com

Regional organization showcasing green building technique, green materials and resource efficiency through community education.

....

New Mexico

Builders Without Borders

Derek Roff, *Director*
119 Main Street
Kingston, NM 88042
505-895-5400
mail@builderswithoutborders.org
www.builderswithoutborders.org
BWB Newsletter; BWB Straw Bale Construction Guide

International network of builders partnering with communities and organizations to provide affordable, ecological housing.

....

New York

Earth Pledge Green Roofs Initiative

Leslie Hoffman, *Director*
122 East 38th Street
New York, NY 10016
212-725-6611
info@earthpledge.org
www.greeninggotham.org
Green Roofs: Ecological Design and Construction

Initiative of Earth Pledge promoting urban green roof development through projects in housing, research and service.

North Carolina

North Carolina Healthy Built Homes Program

Dona Stankus, *Building Programs Manager*
c/o Solar Center
Campus Box 7902
North Carolina State University
Raleigh, NC 27695
513-515-3954
dona_stankus@ncsu.edu
www.healthybuilthomes.org

Regional program providing certification and visibility to homes built using sustainable, high performance practices.

....

Ohio

Oberlin College's Lewis Center for Environmental Studies

Cheryl A. Wolfe-Cragin, *Education Coordinator and Facilities Manager*
AJ Lewis Center 208
Oberlin, OH 44074
440-775-5307
cheryl.wolfe@oberlin.edu
www.oberlin.edu/ajlc/ajlcHome.html

Demonstrative building science and landscape center acting as focus of Oberlin's Environmental Studies program.

....

Ontario

Athena Sustainable Materials Institute

Wayne Trusty, *President*
28 St. John Street
PO Box 189
Merrickville, ON K0G 1N0
613-269-3795
info@athenasmi.ca
www.athenasmi.ca

Not-for-profit organization facilitating research and development activities that leverage environmental considerations in the design process. Developed database, software and resources for life cycle analysis (LCA).

Building Envelope Council Ottawa Region

President
PO Box 7328
Vanier Postal Station, ON K1L 8E4
splescia@cmhc-schl.gc.ca
www.becor.org

Regional not-for-profit organization dedicated to promoting advanced technologies and techniques in building envelope design and construction.

....

Canada Mortgage and Housing Corporation

Program Coordinator
Canada Mortgage and Housing Corporation
700 Montreal Road
Ottawa, ON K1A 0P7
613-748-2000
chic@cmhc-schl.gc.ca
www.cmhc-schl.gc.ca

Program of the Canada Mortgage and Housing Corporation, Canada's national housing agency. Conducts research to promote healthy and sustainable building practices through community outreach and services.

....

Green Roofs for Healthy Cities

Stephen Peck, *Executive Director*
177 Danforth Avenue
Suite 304
Toronto, ON M4K 1N2
416-971-4494
speck@greenroofs.org
www.greenroofs.org

Not-for-profit industry association focused on the development of market opportunities for green roof products and services through community outreach, workshops, research and marketing.

National Roundtable on the Environment and the Economy - National Brownfield Redevelopment Strategy

Sara Melamed, *Special Projects Manager*
344 Slater Street, Suite 200
Ottawa, ON K1R 7Y3
613-995-7519
melameds@nrtee-trnee.ca
Cleaning up the Past, Building the Future: A National Brownfield Redevelopment Strategy for Canada

Federal agency program dedicated to developing a strategy that incorporates both government and private measures to facilitate the redevelopment of brownfields.

....

Natural Resources Canada's Buildings Group

Program Coordinator
CANMET Energy Technology Centre
580 Booth Street, 13th Floor
Ottawa, ON K1A 0E4
http://buildingsgroup.nrcan.gc.ca/home/home_e.asp

Research group dedicated to research and development of advanced technologies that reduce energy consumption and greenhouse gas emission.

....

Seventh Generation Community Projects

Executive Director
1411A Carling Avenue
Suite 202
Ottawa, ON K1Z 1A7
613-233-9880
info@seventhgeneration.ca
www.seventhgeneration.ca
National Capital Region Green Pages

Regional not-for-profit organization promoting sustainable living practices through workshops, community outreach and organizational networking.

Oregon

BetterBricks

Program Director
529 SW Third Avenue
Suite 600
Portland, OR 97204
888-216-5357
info@betterbricks.com
www.betterbricks.com

Regional not-for-profit organization dedicated to promoting energy efficiency through increased awareness, demand and market capability.

....

Earth Advantage

Program Director
16280 SW Upper Boones Ferry Road
Portland, OR 97224
888-327-8433
info@earthadvantage.org
www.earthadvantage.org

Resource center promoting energy efficiency and sustainable design through assisting building professionals.

....

Education for Sustainability Western Network (EFS West)

Julian Dautremont-Smith, *Acting Executive Director*
1935 SE 24th Avenue
Portland, OR 97214
503-222-7041
info@efswest.org
www.efswest.org
Network News

Regional professional association of education professionals and institutions focused on making sustainability a key issue in higher education. The program is a partner of Second Nature.

G/Rated
Terry Miller, *Policy and Programs Coordinator*
721 NW 9th Avenue
Suite 350
Portland, OR 97209
503-823-7418
greenrated@ci.portland.or.us
www.green-rated.org
Green City; G/Rated Tenant Improvement Guide

Regional program of Portland's Office of Sustainable Development providing up-front technical assistance, educational resources, and competitive grants to advance Portland's green building market.

....

Northwest Alliance for Ecological Design Education
Heather Flint, *Co-Chair*
Eugene, OR
alliancenw@yahoo.com

Regional association of students, educators and professionals dedicated to promoting eco-design education and practice at colleges and universities of the northwest.

....

Pennsylvania

ACI (Affordable Comfort)
Linda Wigington, *Manager Program Design and Development*
32 Church Street
Suite 204
Waynesburgh, PA 15370
724-627-5200
lindawig@affordablecomfort.org
www.affordablecomfort.org

Organization advancing residential building performance through the education of building professionals including nationally-known annual and regional conferences.

Green Building Alliance
Rebecca Flora, *Director of Education and Research*
64 S. 14th Street
Pittsburgh, PA 15203
412-431-0709
info@gbapgh.org
www.gbapgh.org
Shades of Green; The Cornerstone

Regional professional organization and USGBC Affiliate integrating environmentally responsible design into the Pittsburgh/Western Pennsylvania building market.

....

Saskatchewan

National Research Council's Centre for Sustainable Infrastructure Research
Dr. David W. Hubble, *Manager*
6 Research Drive, Suite 301
Regina, SK S4S 7J7
306-780-3208
csir-crid@nrc-cnrc.gc.ca
http://irc.nrc-cnrc.gc.ca/csir/index_e.html

Regional organization focused on research and development of sustainable infrastructure technologies.

....

Texas

Austin Energy Green Building Program
Richard Morgan, *Program Manager*
Austin, TX
512-482-5309
richard.morgran@austinenergy.com
www.ci.austin.tx.us/greenbuilder/

Organization dedicated to assisting the building community with sustainable design endeavors. They offer consulting services, seminars, educational events, and publications geared toward residential, commercial and multi-family construction.

Build San Antonio Green
L. Michael Lopez, *Green Program Coordinator*
118 Broadway, Suite 232
San Antonio, TX 78205
210-224-7278
mlopez@buildsagreen.org
www.buildsagreen.org

Joint initiative of the Metropolitan Partnership for Energy and the Greater San Antonio Builders Association focused on creating awareness of resource-efficient building methods, materials and technologies.

....

Sustainable Building Coalition
Program Director
PO Box 49381
Austin, TX 78765
512-663-2927
www.greenbuilder.com/sbc
SBC News

Network of individuals focused on sustainable building, design and development. The Coalition now hosts the Straw Bale Association of Texas (SBAT).

....

Virginia

Arlington Green Home Choice Program
Stella Tarnay, *Arlington County Environmental Planner*
Arlington County Department of Environmental Services
2100 Clarendon Blvd, Suite 900
Arlington, VA 22201
703-228-4792
starnay@arlingtonva.us

Local government program developed to guide and certify the construction of green, energy-efficient homes.

Virginia Sustainable Building Network (VSBN)
Annette Osso, *Executive Director*
Arlington, VA
703-486-2966
vsbn@vsbn.org
www.vsbn.org
VSBN News

Regional not-for-profit organization promoting environmentally sound building practices by facilitating interaction between diverse professional and government sectors.

....

Washington

Built Green Master Builders Association of King & Snohomish Counties
Program Director
335 116th Avenue SE
Bellevue, WA 98004
425-451-7920
builtgreen@mbaks.com
www.builtgreen.net
Built Green News

Regional not-for-profit program of the Master Builders Association of King and Snohomish Counties promoting efficient and environmentally friendly housing.

....

Northwest Eco-Building Guild
Bruce Millard, *President*
PO Box 58530
Seattle, WA 98138
206-575-2222
info@ecobuilding.org
www.ecobuilding.org
NWEBG Green Pages; Eco-Building Times

Regional not-for-profit membership organization advocating environmentally responsible residential and light commercial construction.

Wisconsin

Society of Building Science Educators (SBSE)

Jim Wasley, *President*
University of Wisconsin at Milwaukee
PO Box 413
Milwaukee, WI 53201
jwasley@uwm.edu
www.sbse.org
SBSE News

Association of university educators and practitioners in architecture and related disciplines supporting the teaching of environmental science and building technologies with resources, networking and curriculum research.

Individual Instructors

Individuals and their organizational affiliations here include a selection of those currently offering instruction in ecological design and building as individuals and/or through schools and organizations not listed elsewhere in this book.

Arizona

Arctic Building Consultants
Gerald Goodman
PO Box 403, Ester, AK 99725
907-474-3694
ggg@mosquitonet.com

Instructor focused on strawbale and other methods of construction.

....

Alberta

Autonomous and Sustainable Housing
Jorg Ostrowski
9211 Surfield Drive NW
Calgary, AB T3L 1V9
403-239-1882
jdo@ecobuildings.net
www.ecobuildings.net

Instructors and workshop leaders teaching green building techniques, including passive solar, solar greenhouses, and strawbale.

....

Arizona

Out on Bale, (un)Ltd.
Judy Knox & Matts Mhyrman
1037 E. Linden Street
Tucson, AZ 85719
520-622-5896
mattsmhyrman@aol.com

Instructors and long-time leaders of the strawbale movement.

....

Solar Design and Construction
Ed Dunn
21 W. Pine Avenue
Flagstaff, AZ 86001
928-774-6308
solarbale@cybertrails.com

Instructor, designer and consultant in topics of earth building, sustainable living, strawbale and passive solar construction. Currently the Coconino County Green Building Manger.

California

Bob Theis
6435 Claremont Avenue
Richmond Heights, CA 94805
510-235-0616
bob@bobtheis.net
www.bobtheis.net

Architect and instructor in sustainable design, community planning and Permaculture.

....

Common Sense Design
Pete Gang
145 Keller Street
Petaluma, CA 94952
707-762-4838
pete@commonsensedesign.com
www.commonsensedesign.com

A licensed architect, LEED Accredited Professional, and core faculty member in the Green Building Professional Certificate Program at Sonoma State University. Independent instruction in straw bale construction and other natural building materials and methods.

....

Emerald Earth Sanctuary
Michael G. Smith
PO Box 764, Boonville, CA 95415
707-895-3302
workshops@emeraldearth.org
www.emeraldearth.org/workshops.htm

Instructor and author focused natural building techniques including cob, strawbale, straw-clay, earthen plasters and floors, and round pole framing.

....

Martin Hammer
1348 Hopkins Street
Berkeley, CA 94702
510-525-0525
mfhammer@pacbell.net

Architect and instructor focused on strawbale and other sustainable building practices.

Colorado

Geiger Research Institute of Sustainable Building
Dr. Owen Geiger
Crestone, CO 81131
strawhouses@yahoo.com
www.grisb.org

Instructor and former Director of Builders Without Borders, focused on natural and affordable building techniques. Dr. Geiger is co-author of *Builders Without Borders Straw-Bale Construction Guides*, as well as the founder and director of the Research Institute.

....

District of Columbia

Katrin Scholz-Barth Consulting
Katrin Scholz-Barth
1246 Duncan Place NE
Washington, DC 20002
202-544-8453
katrin@scholz-barth.com
www.scholz-barth.com

Lecturer and consultant in ecological landscape design and green roof technology, teaching a regular course at the University of Pennsylvania.

....

Idaho

University of Idaho
Bruce Haglund
Department of Architecture
PO Box 442451
Moscow, ID 83844-2451
bhaglund@uidaho.edu

Architecture professor, SBSE News editor, and long-time green architecture advocate.

....

Iowa

Y's Natural Building
Brad Young
1004 S. Main Street
Fairfield, IA 52556
641-470-1533
straw@lisco.com

Instructor in strawbale and other natural building techniques.

Louisiana

Louisiana State University
Chris C. Theis
LSU School of Architecture
136 Atkinson Hall
Baton Rouge, LA 70803
225-578-4257
decod6@lsu.edu
www.arch.lsu.edu/Faculty-Theis1.htm

Full Professor of Architecture and Graduate Program Coordinator advocating sustainable design. President-elect of Society for Building Science Educators (SBSE).

....

Maryland

University of Maryland
Julie Gabrielli
School of Architecture, Planning, and Preservation
College Park, MD 20742
301-405-6284
gabrielli@toad.net
www.arch.umd.edu

Architect, consultant, and adjunct faculty member, teaching sustainable design studios and seminars.

....

Massachusetts

Green Space Collaborative
Paul Lacinski
PO Box 107
Ashefield, MA 01330
413-628-3800

Instructor in sustainable design techniques with an emphasis on strawbale design specific to Northeastern climates.

Nacul Center for Ecological Architecture
Tullio Inglese
592 Main Street
Amherst, MA 01002
413-256-8025
tia@nacul.com
www.nacul.com
Architect focused on ecological, local design projects and offering internship opportunities and occasional workshops.

....

New Mexico

The Black Range Lodge and Natural Building Resources
Catherine Wanek and Pete Fust
119 Main Street
Kingston, NM 88042
505-895-5652
cat@blackrangelodge.com
www.blackrangelodge.com

Natural building authors and advocates offering workshops and tours of on-site demonstration projects.

....

Earthship Biotecture
Michael Reynolds
PO Box 1041
Taos, NM 87571
505-751-0462
biotecture@earthship.org
www.earthship.org

Instructor and inventor of the Earthship construction technique using rammed earth tires and passive solar design.

....

Econest Building Company
Robert Laporte & Paula Baker-Laporte
PO Box 864
Tesuque, NM 87574
505-984-2928
paula@bakerlaporte.com
www.econest.com

Designers, builders and instructors focusing on timber frame and clay/straw systems with natural, breathable, non-toxic finishes.

Gourmet Adobe
Carole Crews
HC 78 Box 9811
Ranchos de Taos, NM 87557
505-758-7251

Instructor specializing in earthen plasters, alizes, and natural paints.

....

New York

Cornell University
John R. Elliott
College of Human Ecology
E308 Martha Van Rensselaer Hall
Ithaca, NY 14853-4401
607-255-9714
jre15@cornell.edu

Associate Professor in the Department of Design and Environmental Analysis (DEA) teaching courses in ecological literacy and sustainable design literature.

....

Educating the Educators: A Crash Course on Eco Design
David Bergman & Erika Doering
New York, NY
212-475-3106 / 718-923-0231
bergman@cyberg.com / erikaddes@aol.com
www.eco4edu.net

Seminar leaders dedicated to educating design educators about sustainable design principles and the teaching of those principles.

....

Just Another Way Builder
Clark Sanders
10551 Turnpike Road
East Meredith, NY 13757
607-278-5144

Instructor in sustainable design techniques with an emphasis on strawbale, cob and stone specific to Northeastern climates.

Upstate Woodworking, Inc.
David Vail
100 Park Circle
Rochester, NY 14623
585-292-5697
dvail1@rochester.rr.com

Instructor in sustainable design techniques with an emphasis on strawbale construction and plastering techniques.

....

Nova Scotia

Straw House Herbals
Kim Thompson
13183 Highway 7
Ship Harbour, NS B0J 1Y0
902-845-2750
shipharbour@ns.sympatico.ca
www.naturalbuilding.ca

Instructor focused on natural building design and construction with an emphasis on strawbale construction.

....

Ohio

Harvestbuild Associates, Inc.
Mark Hoberecht
13182 N. Boone Road
Columbia Station, OH 44028
440-236-3344
markh@harvestbuild.com
www.harvestbuild.com

Formal and informal workshops on natural building techniques including strawbale, cob and straw-clay construction.

....

Oberlin College
David Orr
Environmental Studies Program
Oberlin, OH 44074
440-775-8312
david.orr@oberlin.edu
www.oberlin.edu/envs/ajlc/

Professor and Chair of the Environmental Studies Program, best known for his pioneering work on environmental literacy in higher education and the green Adam Joseph Lewis Center building.

Ontario

Harvest Homes
Ben Polley
PO Box 29
Hillsburgh, ON N0B 1Z0
519-242-4681
info@harvesthomes.ca
www.harvesthomes.ca

Instructor in sustainable design techniques with an emphasis on strawbale, and people and planet-friendly material selection.

....

University of Waterloo
Terri Meyer Boake
School of Architecture
7 Melville Street S
Cambridge, ON N1S 2H4
416-636-0031
tboake@uwaterloo.ca

Associate Professor of Architecture and long-time SBSE member who assessed "green" and "potentially green" courses at Waterloo for Greening the Curricula 2004.

....

Oregon

Flying Hammer Productions
Lydia Doleman
4709 SE 64th Street
Portland, OR 97206
503-975-4232
ldoleman@yahoo.com

Instructor in sustainable design techniques with an emphasis on natural materials.

....

IronStraw Group
Michael Thomas
IronStraw Institute
332 SE 3rd Street
Oakland, OR 97562
541-817-5756
info@ironstraw.org
www.ironstraw.org

Instructor focused on strawbale construction.

Pennsylvania

Down to Earth
Sigi Koko
220 W. Langhorne Avenue
Bethlehem, PA 18017
610-868-6350
sigikoko@buildnaturally.com
http://buildnaturally.com

Presenter, hands-on workshop instructor, and consultant focused on healthy and ecologically-sensible design.

....

Joseph Jenkins, Inc
Joe Jenkins
324 Old Beech Road
Grove City, PA 16127
814-786-9085
mail@joseph-jenkins.com
www.joseph-jenkins.com

Instructor and author focused on sustainable waste management and traditional building techniques.

....

Pennsylvania State University
David Riley, PhD
Department of Architectural Engineering
220 Engineering Unit A
University Park, PA 16803
814-863-2079
driley@engr.psu.edu
www.engr.psu.edu/ae/faculty/riley/index.asp

Associate Professor teaching sustainable building methods in coordination with the American Indian Housing Initiative.

....

Quebec

Archibio
Michel Bergeron
10 avenue des Pins Quest
Suite 414
Montreal, QC H2W 1P9
514-985-5734
info@archibio.qc.ca
www.archibio.qc.ca

Instructor on a wide range of techniques and processes involved in designing and building an "ecological house."

Université de Montréal
Daniel Pearl
École d'architecture
Pavillon de la Faculté de l'aménagement
2940, chemin de la Côte-Ste-Catherine
Montréal, QC H3T 1B9
514-343-2096
daniel.pearl@umontreal.ca
www.umontreal.ca

Architecture professor advocating sustainable design and co-organizer of "Greening the Curricula Phase 1" in 2002 and "Greening the Curricula Phase 2" in 2004. Chair of the academic education committee of the Canada Green Building Council (CaGBC).

....

Tennessee

Ecoville Architects
Howard Switzer & Katey Culver
668 Hurricane Creek Road
Linden, TN 37096
931-589-6513
ecoarchitect@direcway.com

Instructors in sustainable design techniques with an emphasis on strawbale.

....

University of Tennessee
Mark DeKay
College of Architecture and Design
1715 Volunteer Boulevard
Knoxville, TN 37996
865-974-3249
mdekay@utk.edu
www.sunwindlight.net

Associate Professor in Architecture and sustainable design advocate.

....

Texas

Benjamin Obregon Architects
Ben Obregon
13429 Overland Pass
Austin, TX 78738
512-263-0177
bobregon@austin.rr.com

Architect and instructor in sustainable design techniques with an emphasis on strawbale, passive solar and regionally responsive design.

Norm Ballinger
Austin, TX
512-912-8576
n_ballinger@yahoo.com

Instructor focused on strawbale construction and building code compliance.

....

Thangmaker Construction
Frank Meyer
904 E. Monroe Street
Austin, TX 78704
512-916-8100
thangmaker@aol.com
www.thangmaker.com

Consultant and instructor in sustainable design techniques with an emphasis on straw bale, earthen plasters and floors, bamboo and round timber framing.

....

Utah

OkOkOk Productions
Kaki Hunter & Doni Kiffmeyer
256 E. 100 South
Moab, UT 84532
435-259-8378
okokok@frontiernet.net
www.ok-ok-ok.com

Instructors focused on earthbag construction and earthen and lime plaster selection, mixing and application. Authors of *Earthbag Building*.

....

w/Gaia Design
Susie Harrington
PO Box 264
Moab, UT 84532
435-259-7073
susie@withgaia.com
www.withgaia.org

Architect, landscape architect and instructor in sustainable design techniques with an emphasis on passive solar and alternative materials.

Washington

Living Shelter Design
Terry Phelan
320 Newport Way NW
Issaquah, WA 98027
425-427-8643
info@livingshelter.com
www.livingshelter.com

Architect and instructor in sustainable design techniques.

....

TerraSol Design and Building
Bruce Glenn
1044 Water Street
PMB 231
Port Townsend, WA 98368
360-385-5477
bruce@strawbalehomes.com
www.strawbalehomes.com

Designer, builder, and instructor in natural building techniques and solar design.

Bibliography

#

2004 Green Building Survey [online, cited March 28, 2005]. Environmental Career Center, November 2004.

A

Association of Collegiate Schools of Architecture, *Guide to Architecture Schools*, 7th Edition, 2004.

B

Baniassad, Esmail, "Sustainable Design Education in the Current Architecture Curriculum: Points of Consensus from the Round Table," *ACSA News* Volume 30, Number 9. Association of Collegiate Schools of Architecture, May 2001, pp. 5, 10-11.

Boniface, Russell, "Here Comes the Sun: Decathlon Heats Up Solar Awareness" [online, cited March 28, 2005]. *AIArchitect This Week*, February 14, 2005.

Brown, Antony, "*An operational model for teaching sustainable design*." Ecosa Institute, 2001.

Brown, Reidy, "Sustainable Architecture" [online, cited April 8, 2005].

Butler, Peg, "The Need for Ecological Thinking in Design Education," *Solar Incidents*, Vol. 3 No. 3. University of Oregon, Spring 1998, pp. 1, 4.

C

Cooper, Gina, "Emerging Green Builders: Opening Doors for Young Professionals", *National Environmental Employment Report*, Volume XI Number 8. Environmental Career Center, November 2004, p. 5.

Cooper, Gina, "The State of Sustainable Design and Development Careers: Insight and Inspiration from USGBC President," *National Environmental Employment Report* Volume X Number 6. Environmental Career Center, December 2003, p. 5.

D

E

Ecotone Publishing, "The Philosophy of Sustainable Design: Introduction to Green Architecture Curriculum Pilot Project," 2004.

Ecotone Publishing, *Who's Green 2006: The Directory of Who's Green in the Design and Construction Field*, forthcoming late-2005.

Elizabeth, Lynne and Cassandra Adams eds., *Alternative Construction: Contemporary Natural Building Methods*. John Wiley & Sons, 2000, Revised Edition 2005.

Elliot, Jack, "Learning to Use LEED: One Class's Experience" [online, cited March 28, 2005]. *Metropolis Magazine*, March 29, 2004.

Elliot, Jack, "Teaching Sustainability to Tomorrow's Interior Designers" [online, cited March 28, 2005]. *Metropolis Magazine*, March 22, 2004.

F

Fisher, Thomas, "The Needs of Sustainability," *ACSA News*, Volume 30, Number 1. Association of Collegiate Schools of Architecture, September 2000, pp. 6-7.

Fraker, Harrison, Jr., FAIA, "Is Sustainable Design Still Marginalized in the Schools?" *ACSA News*, Volume 30, Number 3. Association of Collegiate Schools of Architecture, November 2000, pp. 1, 5, 10.

G

Glyphis, John P., ed., *How Can the Architect Contribute to a Sustainable World?* Second Nature, Inc., Wingspread Conference Proceedings, February 2002.

Gould, Kira, "Teaching Green at ICFF 2002" [online, cited March 28, 2005]. *Metropolis Magazine*, May 2002.

"Green Dialogues: Talk About Sustainability!" [online, cited March 28, 2005]. *Metropolis Magazine* – Metropolis West Conference Proceedings, October 2001.

H

Haglund, Bruce, ed., "The Buzz: SBSE Takes on LEED," *SBSE News*, Society of Building Science Educators, Fall 2004, pp. 4-5.

I

J

Jones, Louise, Ph.D., Dorothy L. Fowles, Ph.D., and Elizabeth A. King, Ph.D., "The Mandate for Green/Sustainable Design: Good for People – Good for the Planet Earth" [online, cited March 28, 2005]. *Design for the 21st Century III International Conference on Universal Design* – Conference Proceedings, December 7-12, 2004.

K

Kennedy, Joseph F, Michael G. Smith and Catherine Wanek, eds., *The Art of Natural Building*. New Society Publishers, 2002.

Kwok, Alison, "Agents of Architectural Change," *Architecture Week*, April 2001.

L

Leibowitz, Sandra, *Alternative Careers in Ecological Architecture*, Department of Architecture graduate terminal research project, University of Oregon, 1996.

Leibowitz, Sandra, "Eco-Building Schools: Alternative Educational Resources in Environmentally-Sensitive Building," *Solar Incidents*, Vol. 5 No. 1. University of Oregon, Fall 1994, pp. 1-2, 5.

Leibowitz, Sandra, *Eco-Building Schools: A Directory of Alternative Educational Resources in Environmentally Sensitive Design and Building in the United States*. Self-published, Fall 1996.

Loftness, Vivian, AIA, "Carnegie Mellon is Committed to Sustainability – What About You?" *ACSA News* Volume 30, Number 2. Association of Collegiate Schools of Architecture, October 2000, pp. 6, 9.

M

Magwood, Chris. “Getting Trained in Strawbale and Natural Building”, *The Last Straw*, Issue #47. Green Prairie Foundation for Sustainability, Fall 2004, pp. 4-9.

Magwood, Chris. “Teaching Natural Building to Youth.” *The Last Straw*, Issue #47. Green Prairie Foundation for Sustainability, Fall 2004, pp. 9-10.

Malin, Nadav, “Architecture Schools Now Required to Teach Sustainable Design,” *Environmental Building News*, Vol. 14, No. 4. Building Green, April 2005, pp. 3-4.

McDonald, Margot, ed., *SEDE: Sustainable Environmental Design Education* [online, cited March 28, 2005].

McDonough, William, “Teaching Design That Goes From Cradle to Cradle” [online, cited September 6, 2004]. *The Chronicle Review*, July 23, 2004.

McLennan, Jason, and Peter Rumsey, “Green Edge: The Greening of Education”, *Environmental Design + Construction*. November 2004, pp. 126-7.

McLennan, Jason, *The Philosophy of Sustainable Design*, Ecotone Publishing Company, 2004.

Mitchell, William J., “E-Green”, *ACSA News* Volume 30, Number 8. April 2001, p. 5.

N

National Architectural Accrediting Board, *NAAB Conditions for Accreditation for Professional Degree Programs in Architecture*, 2004 Edition.

O

Orr, David, *Ecological Literacy: Education and the Transition To A Postmodern World*. State University of New York Press, 1992.

P

Pearl, Daniel, “Greening the Curricula Phase 2: Words to Action”, April 2004.

Q

R

Rosenman, Marvin and Joseph Bilello, eds., *EASE: Educating Architects for a Sustainable Environment*. [online, cited April 6, 2005].

S

Sanders, Linda, FAIA, “Following Nature’s Lead: The California Power Crisis and Sustainable Design”, *ACSA News* Volume 30, Number 7. Association of Collegiate Schools of Architecture, March 2001, pp. 5, 27.

Schwartz, Keara, “Understanding and Evaluating Sustainability at Carnegie Mellon University” [online, cited March 28, 2005]. *Metropolis Magazine*, 2004.

Southface Energy Institute, “Southface: A place to grow and learn,” *National Environmental Employment Report* Volume X Number 6. Environmental Career Center, December 2003, p. 7.

"Survey Released on Career Trends in Green Building," *National Environmental Employment Report Volume* XI Number 7. Environmental Career Center, September 2004, p. 6.

Szenasy, Susan S., "Sustainable Pedagogies and Practices" [online, cited March 28, 2005]. *Metropolis Magazine* – Keynote Address from ACSA/AIA Teachers' Seminar, June 2003.

Szenasy, Susan S., ed., "Teaching Green: Full Survey Report" [online, cited March 28, 2005]. *Metropolis Magazine*, May 2002.

Szenasy, Susan S., ed., "School Survey 2003: Taking the pulse of sustainable design education in North America" [online, cited March 28, 2005]. *Metropolis Magazine*, August 2003.

T

Tanzer, Kim, "Strengthening NAAB Criteria to Reflect a Commitment to the Principles of Sustainability within Architectural Curricula." Open memorandum to Sharon Matthews, Executive Director, NAAB, August 22, 2003.

Theis, Christopher, "Prospects for Ecological Design Education." Paper presented at Society of Building Science Educators Annual Retreat, June 2002.

Theis, Christopher, "Retreat 2005 – Greener Foundations: Environmental Technology and the Beginning Design Student," *SBSE News*, Society of Building Science Educators, Winter 2004, pp. 1, 4.

Thomson Peterson's, *Graduate Programs in Arts and Architecture 2004*, 4th Edition.

U

V

Van der Ryn, Sim and Stuart Cowen, *Ecological Design*, Island Press, 1996.

W

Wheelwright, Peter M., "Texts and Lumps: Thoughts on Science and Sustainability," *ACSA News* Volume 30, Number 4. Association of Collegiate Schools of Architecture, December 2000, pp. 5-6.

Wasley, Jim, "SBSE Green Curricula Inventory," *SBSE News*, Society of Building Science Educators, Fall 2002, p. 2.

Wilson, Alex, ed., "Sustainability in Architectural Education." *Environmental Building News*, Vol. 9 No. 7/8. Building Green, July/August 2000, p. 8.

X

Y

Z

Index of Listings

This index includes, alphabetically by name, the Schools, Curriculum Resources, Related Organizations, and Individual Instructors listed in their respective sections of this book. Individual Instructors are listed in this index both by individual last name and by affiliation, where applicable.

Cleveland Green Building Coalition		
Schools Directory	Cleveland	Ohio
Cob Cottage Company		
Schools Directory	Cottage Grove	Oregon
Cobworks		
Schools Directory	Mayne Island	British Columbia
Colorado State University at Fort Collins		
Schools Directory	Fort Collins	Colorado
Colorado Straw Bale Association (COSBA)		
Related Organizations	Boulder	Colorado
Common Sense Design		
Individual Instructors	Petaluma	California
Cornell University		
Individual Instructors	Ithaca	New York
Crews, Carole (Gourmet Adobe)		
Individual Instructors	Ranchos de Taos	New Mexico
Culver, Katey (Ecoville Architects)		
Individual Instructors	Linden	Tennessee
Curriculum Information Database (SBSE)		
Curriculum Resources	Milwaukee	Wisconsin
D		
DAWN Southwest		
Schools Directory	Tucson	Arizona
Dekay, Mark (U. of Tennessee)		
Individual Instructors	Knoxville	Tennessee
Development Center for Appropriate Technology (DCAT)		
Related Organizations	Tucson	Arizona
Doering, Erika (Educating the Educators)		
Individual Instructors	New York	New York
Doleman, Lydia (Flying Hammer Productions)		
Individual Instructors	Portland	Oregon
Down to Earth		
Individual Instructors	Bethlehem	Pennsylvania
Dunn, Ed (Solar Design and Construction)		
Individual Instructors	Flagstaff	Arizona
E		
Earth Advantage		
Related Organizations	Portland	Oregon
Earth Pledge Green Roofs Initiative		
Related Organizations	New York	New York
Earthship Biotecture		
Individual Instructors	Taos	New Mexico
Earthwood Building School		
Schools Directory	West Chazy	New York
Eco-Broker		
Schools Directory	Evergreen	Colorado
Ecological Design Institute		
Related Organizations	Sausalito	California
Ecological Literacy in Architectural Education (AIA)		
Curriculum Resources	Washington	District of Columbia
Econest Building Company		
Individual Instructors	Tesuque	New Mexico
Ecosa Institute		
Schools Directory	Prescott	Arizona
EcoVersity		
Schools Directory	Santa Fe	New Mexico

Greater Vancouver Regional District's BuildSmart		
Related Organizations	Burnaby	British Columbia
Green Advantage		
Schools Directory	Taylorstown	Virginia
Green Architecture Curriculum Project (Ecotone)		
Curriculum Resources	Kansas City	Missouri
Green Building Alliance		
Related Organizations	Pittsburgh	Pennsylvania
Green Building Institute at the Envirocenter		
Related Organizations	Glen Burnie	Maryland
Green Buildings BC		
Related Organizations	Vancouver	British Columbia
Green Design Education Initiative		
Curriculum Resources	N/A	N/A
Green Points Program		
Related Organizations	Boulder	Colorado
Green Prairie Foundation for Sustainability		
Related Organizations	Lincoln	Nebraska
Green Roofs for Healthy Cities		
Related Organizations	Toronto	Ontario
The Green Roundtable, Inc. (GRT)		
Related Organizations	Cambridge	Massachusetts
Green Space Collaborative		
Individual Instructors	Ashefield	Massachusetts
GreenHOME, Inc.		
Related Organizations	Washington	District of Columbia
Greening the Curricula / Verdir le Diplôme		
Curriculum Resources	N/A	N/A
Groundworks		
Schools Directory	Murphy	Oregon
H		
Haglund, Bruce (U. of Idaho)		
Individual Instructors	Moscow	Idaho
Hammer, Martin		
Individual Instructors	Berkeley	California
Harrington, Susie (w/Gaia Design)		
Individual Instructors	Moab	Utah
Harvest Homes		
Individual Instructors	Hillsburgh	Ontario
HarvestBuild Associates, Inc.		
Individual Instructors	Columbia Station	Ohio
Healthy Building Network		
Related Organizations	Washington	District of Columbia
Heartwood School for the Homebuilding Crafts		
Schools Directory	Washington	Massachusetts
Hoberecht, Mark (HarvestBuild Assoc.)		
Individual Instructors	Columbia Station	Ohio
House Alive		
Schools Directory	Jacksonville	Oregon
Hunter, Kaki (OkOkOk Productions)		
Individual Instructors	Moab	Utah
I		
Inglese, Tullio (Nacul Center)		
Individual Instructors	Amherst	Massachusetts
Institute for Sustainable Power		
Related Organizations	Highlands Ranch	Colorado

Mid-America Straw Bale Association (MASBA) - see Green Prairie Foundation for Sustainability	Lincoln	Nebraska
Related Organizations		
Mississippi State University	Starkville	Mississippi
Schools Directory		
Montgomery College	Rockville	Maryland
Schools Directory		
N		
Nacul Center for Ecological Architecture		
Individual Instructors	Amherst	Massachusetts
National Association of Home Builders (NAHB) Research Center		
Related Organizations	Upper Marlboro	Maryland
National Center for Appropriate Technology (NCAT)		
Related Organizations	Butte	Montana
National Institute of Building Sciences		
Related Organizations	Washington	District of Columbia
National Research Council's Centre for Sustainable Infrastructure Research		
Related Organizations	Regina	Saskatchewan
National Round Table on the Environment and the Economy - National Brownfield Redevelopment Strategy		
Related Organizations	Ottawa	Ontario
Natural Resources Canada's Buildings Group		
Related Organizations	Ottawa	Ontario
Natural Resources Canada's Office of Energy Efficiency - Buildings Programs		
Related Organizations	Ottawa	Ontario
NCARB Monographs		
Curriculum Resources	Washington	District of Columbia
New College of California		
Schools Directory	Santa Rosa	California
North Carolina Healthy Built Homes Program		
Related Organizations	Raleigh	North Carolina
Northeast Sustainable Energy Association (NESEA)		
Related Organizations	Greenfield	Massachusetts
Northwest Alliance for Ecological Design Education		
Related Organizations	Eugene	Oregon
Northwest Eco-Building Guild		
Related Organizations	Seattle	Washington
O		
Obergon, Benjamin (Benjamin Obregon Architects)		
Individual Instructors	Austin	Texas
Oberlin College		
Individual Instructors	Oberlin	Ohio
Oberlin College's Lewis Center for Environmental Studies		
Related Organizations	Oberlin	Ohio
Occidental Arts and Ecology Center		
Schools Directory	Occidental	California
Ocean Arks International		
Related Organizations	Falmouth	Massachusetts
OkOkOk Productions		
Individual Instructors	Moab	Utah
One United Resource Ecovillage		
Schools Directory	Shawnigan Lake	British Columbia
Orr, David (Oberlin College)		
Individual Instructors	Oberlin	Ohio
Ostrowski, Jorg (ASH)		
Individual Instructors	Calgary	Alberta

Out on Bale, (un)Ltd.		
Individual Instructors	Tucson	Arizona
P		
Pacific Gas & Electric's Pacific Energy Center		
Schools Directory	San Francisco	California
Pacific Gas & Electric's Stockton Energy Training Center		
Schools Directory	Stockton	California
Pangea Partnership, The		
Schools Directory	Ottawa	Ontario
Partnership for Advancing Technology in Housing (PATH)		
Related Organizations	Washington	District of Columbia
Pearl, Daniel (U. de Montréal)		
Individual Instructors	Montreal	Quebec
Penn State University		
Individual Instructors	University Park	Pennsylvania
Phelan, Terry (Living Shelter Design)		
Individual Instructors	Issaquah	Washington
Polley, Ben (Harvest Homes)		
Individual Instructors	Hillsburgh	Ontario
Portland Community College		
Schools Directory	Portland	Oregon
R		
RedVector.com		
Curriculum Resources	Tampa	Florida
Report Card on Ecological Design Education (NWAEDE)		
Curriculum Resources	Eugene	Oregon
Reynolds, Michael (Earthship Biotecture)		
Individual Instructors	Taos	New Mexico
Riley, David (Penn State U.)		
Individual Instructors	University Park	Pennsylvania
Rocky Mountain Institute		
Related Organizations	Snowmass	Colorado
Rocky Mountain Workshops		
Schools Directory	Fort Collins	Colorado
S		
Sage Mountain Center		
Related Organizations	Whitehall	Montana
San Francisco Institute of Architecture		
Schools Directory	Alameda	California
Sanders, Clark (Just Another Way Builder)		
Individual Instructors	East Meredith	New York
Scholz-Barth, Katrin (Katrin Scholz-Barth Consulting)		
Individual Instructors	Washington	District of Columbia
Scottsdale Green Building Program		
Related Organizations	Scottsdale	Arizona
Seattle Central Community College		
Schools Directory	Seattle	Washington
Second Nature		
Related Organizations	Boston	Massachusetts
Seven Generations Natural Builders		
Schools Directory	Bolinas	California
Seventh Generation Community Projects		
Related Organizations	Ottawa	Ontario
Shaw EcoVillage		
Schools Directory	Washington	District of Columbia

Shelter Institute		
Schools Directory	Woolwich	Maine
Sir Sandford Fleming College		
Schools Directory	Haliburton	Ontario
Smith, Michael G. (Emerald Earth Sanctuary)		
Individual Instructors	Boonville	California
Society of Building Science Educators (SBSE)		
Related Organizations	Milwaukee	Wisconsin
Solar Design and Construction		
Individual Instructors	Flagstaff	Arizona
Solar Energy International		
Schools Directory	Carbondale	Colorado
Solar Living Institute		
Schools Directory	Hopland	California
Sonoma State University		
Schools Directory	Rohnert Park	California
Southface Energy Institute		
Schools Directory	Atlanta	Georgia
Southwest Solar Adobe School		
Schools Directory	Bosque	New Mexico
Straw Bale Association of Nebraska (SBAN) - (Green Prairie Foundation for Sustainability)		
Related Organizations	Lincoln	Nebraska
Straw House Herbals		
Individual Instructors	Ship Harbour	Nova Scotia
Strawbale Association of Texas - see Sustainable Building Coalition		
Related Organizations	Austin	Texas
Sustainable Building Coalition		
Related Organizations	Austin	Texas
Sustainable Buildings Industry Council		
Related Organizations	Washington	District of Columbia
Sustainable Environmental Design Education (SEDE, Cal Poly San Luis Obispo)		
Curriculum Resources	San Luis Obispo	California
Sustainable Facilities & Infrastructure Program (Georgia Tech Research Institute)		
Curriculum Resources	Atlanta	Georgia
Sustainable Systems Support		
Individual Instructors	Bisbee	Arizona
Switzer, Howard (Ecoville Architects)		
Individual Instructors	Linden	Tennessee
T		
TerraSol Design and Building		
Individual Instructors	Port Townsend	Washington
Thangmaker Construction		
Individual Instructors	Austin	Texas
The Last Straw Journal		
Related Organizations	Lincoln	Nebraska
Theis, Bob		
Individual Instructors	Richmond Heights	California
Theis, Chris C. (Louisiana State U.)		
Individual Instructors	Baton Rouge	Louisiana
Thomas, Michael (IronStraw Group)		
Individual Instructors	Oakland	Oregon
Thompson, Kim (Strawhouse Herbals)		
Individual Instructors	Ship Harbour	Nova Scotia
Timber Framers Guild		
Schools Directory	Becket	Massachusetts

Wright Way Organic Resource Center Schools Directory	Mailbu	California
Y		
Yestermorrow Design/Build School Schools Directory	Warren	Vermont
Young, Brad (Y's Natural Building) Individual Instructors	Fairfield	Iowa
Y's Natural Building Individual Instructors	Fairfield	Iowa

About the Author

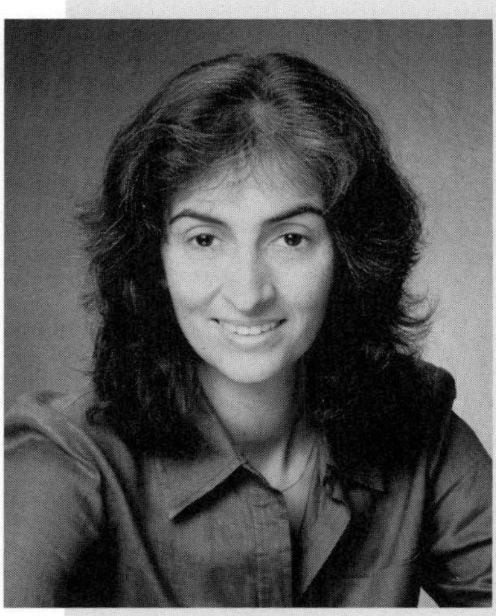

Sandra Leibowitz Earley is an architect who focuses on greener solutions for the built environment. She holds a Master of Architecture degree from the University of Oregon, where she concentrated in sustainable design, while complimenting it with various unconventional ecological design and building coursework. Drawing from this broad educational base, she has continuously pursued and helped advance this emerging field as a professional. She founded Sustainable Design Consulting, with offices in Richmond, Virginia and Silver Spring, Maryland, to provide a range of green building services for commercial, institutional and multi-family residential projects.

In addition to project consulting, Ms. Earley writes and presents on a variety of ecological design and building subjects. She has authored and co-authored several articles and guidance documents, including the 1998 edition of the *HOK Sustainable Design Guide*, the 1999 edition of *GreenSpec* and the *U.S. Green Building Council Toolkit for State and Local Governments*. This most recent publication, *Ecological Design and Building Schools* substantially updates and expands her 1996 self-publication, *Eco-Building Schools*.

About New Village Press

You are holding one of the first titles from New Village Press, the only publisher to focus on the emerging field of sustainable grassroots community building. Through illustrated profiles and teaching and resource guides, New Village offers proven solutions to seemingly intractable environmental, social and economic challenges. Our publications cross boundaries between academic and informal education, with non-fiction books that span the fields of architecture and planning, ecology, economic development, social justice, arts and culture.

The Press is a project of Architects / Designers / Planners for Social Responsibility (ADPSR), an educational non-profit organization working for peace, environmental protection, ecological building, social justice, and the development of healthy communities. ADPSR believes that design practitioners have a significant role to play in the well-being of our communities. Visit www.adpsr.org

New Village Press has three aditional Fall 2005 releases:

- ***Beginner's Guide to Community-Based Arts***, ten graphic stories about artists, educators, and activists across the United States.
- ***Works of HeART***, a full-color celebration of citizen artists revitalizing their communities.
- ***Doing Time in the Garden***, the only comprehensive guide to creating in-prison and post-release horticultural training programs.

Look for future titles on ecological schoolyards, community gardens and the commons, community-based arts, and restorative alternatives to prison.

New Village books are distributed to the trade by Consortium Book Sales and Distribution. For further information about individual titles, authors and how to purchase books, visit **www.newvillagepress.net**

newvillagePRESS

320008